AF407934

Suzana Sjenicic
Anxiety Free

Graphic Design
Andjelija Krstic

Photography
Goran Veljic

Interior Design
Marina Markovic

Other Works by Author:
Oslobodjeni anksioznosti
(Anxiety Free – Serbian Edition)

Suzana Sjenicic

Anxiety Free

TABLE OF CONTENTS

Introduction 6

   Mom 8

   Denial 10

   But, what happened to the family? 12

   Teamwork 16

   Graduation 18

Anxiety 19

   Symptoms 20

   Types of anxiety 25

Anxiety from my angle 28

   Know your triggers 30

   Exposure to fears 31

Coping strategies 33

   Awareness/mindfulness 33

   Automatic thought record (ATR) 36

   Breathing 37

   Meditation 39

Journaling 46

Lists 49

Your cognitions 58

Circle of control...61

Prayer...63

Pets 66

Be judgement-free 69

Stop bottling up!..72

Charge your "phone".....................................75

Value of a minute...78

Decluttering 82

Get creative..85

Coloring books 89

Visualization..89

Physical activity...94

Support..100

Power of the will..101

Closing remarks 102

INTRODUCTION

Disclaimer: This is NOT another typical self-help book. Although, yes, I will admit that many of, well, all of the things I'm writing about will be helpful to you, and you will be able to apply them (pause for reaction) YOURSELF. But, I am not writing this book solely as a psychotherapist – in fact, that is probably the least reason why I picked it up. I want to write as a person, as somebody who experienced anxiety on multiple levels in her life; first hand, and as a care taker of my mother. And today, I am grateful for it. I want to share my story with you, in hopes that we can speak about anxiety without stigma, learn to support one another, cope with it, and know that we are not alone. Anxiety is more common than you think, but it is also probably one of the most difficult disorders to accept and live with.

When I say that I am grateful, I mean that it taught me so much, and it made me a better person and a better psycho-therapist. Having experienced it, I know what it feels like and it is easy for me to relate to my patients who are struggling with it. Having been a care taker of somebody who is still struggling, made me aware of how difficult that is for the loved ones of the anxious person, and how much impact anxiety has on a vast circle of people around the patient. Having been there, I learned the thought processes, explored relationships between thoughts and feelings, feelings and physical reactions, thoughts and physical reactions. It is fascinating to realize how much power is hidden in one tiny thought; but also, begin to understand that we are the ones who have the control over it. I learned that I could start and stop my own anxiety as I wished, a skill that is difficult to master, but operates on a simple principle. I will discuss this more in the upcoming chapters.

Before I continue with my story and start telling you what to do, it is only fair to introduce myself and tell you who I am, so you can decide whether it's even worth reading what I have to say. I am a psychotherapist, more precisely, Licensed Mental Health Counselor in the State of New York, and I currently work in a private practice, working with a variety of clients with distinct mental health issues, most of all anxiety and related disorders. Over time, I realized that almost every patient of mine has some anxiety, no matter what the diagnosis – and who in the world doesn't, and on a daily basis? I find that I effectively work with anxiety disorders, maybe because of my own experiences, but maybe because of my great interest in it and curiosity about further studying and exploring different treatment options. I find anxiety to be one of the most rewarding disorders to work with, as it is amazing to observe the positive change in the patient, as I help them on their journey towards liberating themselves from faulty cognitions. This is how I got there.

MOM

April 23rd, 2014. I was working at the Office for Students with Disabilities at LaGuardia Community College in Long Island City, New York, as a counseling intern and a Master Tutor. I accepted that position upon finishing my Bachelor's degree at the New York University, while I was applying the to the Mental Health Counseling Master's programs. I continued to work there throughout my first year of Master's at The Bernard M. Baruch College, and was able to add some hours to complete my practicum at the same office as required by the program. I was very busy at the time, given that the program was a full-time cohort model, required four full days of classes, and a practicum which turns into a full-time internship in the second year. It was nearly impossible to work at the same time, but I was lucky to be able to do both at the same place by only extending my work day by a few hours as practicum required only 100 per semester.

On that 23rd of April, my phone rang while I was working at my desk in between sessions with students. It was my mom; she never called during my work or school hours, she'd usually text me. I felt something was wrong. I picked up the phone, and listened as she was barely able to articulate between heavy, shallow breaths, "Come home, I am not feeling well." She hung up and I called my father who worked at the same college to drive us home immediately.

It took us about 15 minutes to get home – it felt like an eternity. We walked in and mom was sitting in her favorite armchair, pale, hyperventilating, blood pressure machine next to her. She was barely able to speak. I asked her about what has happened and what she was feeling, and she told me that her blood pressure was high, that her heart was beating fast, she couldn't breathe, and was experiencing chest pains and numbness in her left arm. "Please let it not be a heart attack," I thought, and without thinking dialed 911.

The paramedics came within minutes and while one was taking her blood pressure and performing EKG, the other stood by the door collecting insurance information and commented, "She's anxious." Dad and I looked at her as if she was crazy. Of course she's anxious, she may be having a heart attack. The paramedic continued to say that she's had a panic attack and is fine. She was so sure about it, that she did not even make a recommendation for further testing at the hospital. I was puzzled. "But I am studying this, how come I didn't recognize it? No, it's impossible for mom to have it… Heart disease runs in her family too, we better check it out. She's never had anxiety before…" My brain was going 100 mph. Mom felt better and that's what mattered. However, it did not stop me from immediately scheduling all possible appointments, starting from her primary physician, to the cardiologist, to the endocrinologist, and every other "gist" I could think of. It was difficult to admit that the only "gist" she needed was a psychologist.

DENIAL

One of the greatest struggles with any kind of mental health disorder is admitting that the person has it. In our society, no matter how much we hope that stigma is alleviated, it is difficult to accept that one is suffering from a mental health issue, even if it's anxiety. Somehow, it is easier to accept another medical problem that is physical. As if the difference between mind and body is so significant, that one is embarrassing and the other is not. In recent years we all started talking about stigma and fighting against it, yet when somebody suffers from mental illness, we find it difficult to talk about. As a therapist, I could talk about this for days, but I won't; we all got the point. I will, however, say that I am always proud of seeing and hearing people talk about their mental illness publicly, and nonchalantly as it is a perfectly normal part of them – because it is. It is always heartwarming to hear somebody say, "Yes, I have anxiety" with a smile on their face because they got it under control and accepted it as a part of their daily life.

One thing I strongly disagree with though is the connotation that mental illness describes the person. "She is anxious." "He is schizophrenic." "He is depressed." She is bipolar." No. People struggling with mental illness ARE NOT mental illness; they just have it. It is a part of them, but it does not describe their persona. There is so much more to these people than their diagnosis – believe me. I have/had the pleasure of working with and knowing so many wonderful, successful artists, businessmen/businesswomen, teachers, fellow therapists, and students with so many lovely layers to their personalities. Mental struggles were just one tiny bit of who they are. As a matter of fact, I live with one of those wonderful women whose anxiety is just one small part of her.

I want to say something that might clash with what I have talked about until now, but it is the truth and we all know it. Denial is big. Sometimes the denial of family is greater than that of the person struggling with mental illness. I was the first one to deny, to look for other answers, because remember? Physical medical explanation is a more acceptable option. I could not admit that my mother, MY MOTHER, struggled with anxiety. I was just finishing my first year of the Mental Health Counseling master's program, and I would've seen it, for God's sakes! The truth is, I didn't want to see it. After so many "gists" examined mom (the search for the medical explanation lasted for about 3 months) and every single one of them concluded that she was anxious by taking just one look at her, after all the tests came back clear, and after I finally took her to the psychotherapist, I began to make my own peace with it. I admitted to myself that yes, it could happen to my family, and no, there is nothing I can do about it but support her. That was the beginning of our journey. I, as a therapist who happened to be a daughter, have had my hands tied. I helped with small suggestions, worked with mom on deep breathing, got her to meditate and do yoga, but I could not "cure" her. I had to let go and allow somebody else to do the job. I always think back to somebody who said, "The dentist cannot fix his own teeth, can he? A heart surgeon cannot operate on his own heart, right?" A therapist could not help her own mother.

BUT, WHAT HAPPENED TO THE FAMILY?

Living with mental illness, as "minor" as anxiety, is difficult for the person experiencing it. Just as difficult, if not more so, it becomes for those living with them, particularly the main caretaker. I did not talk much about symptoms of anxiety yet, but will get into that shortly. What I want to talk about is how taxing it is to live with it daily. Overall mood changes, tension within the household, frequent arguments, and believe it, or not – transmitted symptoms of anxiety, especially if you happen to be very close to the person struggling with it.

My family has always been very close, very strong, especially during difficult times. We always stick together, no matter what is going on; and this time, it was no different. Mom's anxiety was getting more and more severe, panic attacks would happen almost daily, and it all became very debilitating for all of us. Dad didn't know what to do, so most of the work was done by me. He would help with making juices, lemonades, wet cloths for mom's forehead, but I would then send him to sleep so at least one of us could go to work functioning the next day, and so that he could take over when we come back from work, so I could, possibly, if nothing major is going on, take a nap. I can't tell you how many times I had gone to work running on two hours of sleep.

I can't tell you how many nights we spent at emergency rooms because her blood pressure would spike so much and cause even more anxiety because of her allergy to the blood pressure medications (among so many others, which greatly contributed to her health-related anxiety). It got to the point where dad and I began to joke about it, saying that we are going out on a nightly basis, taking a ride to the hospital to see what's up and coming back home. We'd spend hours waiting only for the doctors to repeat to us that it was all just severe anxiety, and dismiss us from the hospital. Mom would feel better the moment we got there, only knowing that she is in the safe place, and of course, by the time we made it to the hospital, panic attack would begin to subside.

As mom was diagnosed with anxiety officially in May, my semester at school was almost over which worked out well; there was no school related sacrifice. However, when the summer arrived, I was unable to leave home. Mom developed dependency on me due to her lack of knowledge of English, fear of being alone, and health anxiety, which caused panic every time I was too far from home. As the time went on, I became tired of feeling anxious myself whenever I'd leave the house – I'd constantly hold my phone in my hand, worry about how she is doing and whether the phone will ring letting me know that she is anxious again - and having to run home immediately so I can tend to her, so it finally became easier for me to just stay in and have some peace.

Unfortunately, and I feel guilty even saying that, I started to feel resentful towards the situation (never towards mom as it was not her choice, although, I do have to admit annoyance in my voice when she asked for something, reported symptoms of anxiety that were coming up again, or even talked about it to other people in my presence). I missed out on going out with my friends, spending the summer at the beach, and relaxing in general before school started again. I was constantly tired and irritable, worried and wondering – will this ever be over? My only outings during that summer were various doctors' visits, as I had spent a lot of the time trying to find her psychotherapists, acupuncturists, naturopaths, and other professionals who might be able to help her. Vast amount of my time was spent teaching her breathing techniques, looking for suitable meditations, and introducing her to various behavioral approaches that would, hopefully, lessen her anxiety.

My nervousness about the beginning of the school year in-creased rapidly as we dipped our toes into August. How would I attend classes? We quickly decided to fly in my grandma from Europe to spend at least three months with mom, while I finish the semester; then, we hoped, things will get better so I can push through the whole school year. We had to think day by day, there was no planning ahead. Grandma came, and somehow, mom was somewhat comfortable with her. Mother is a mother, I guess, and knows how to deal with her child – regardless of that child's age. Surprisingly, I didn't miss out on school as much as I thought I would. I'd get an occasional phone call and had to leave before the end of the last class, at times, I'd miss the first morning class, and sometimes, I was forced to miss the entire day because we just had a bad night and a worse morning. All in all, I somehow managed to push through the semester and get good grades.

School became my escape. Reality was too painful to be present in, so I found my peace in the books. I studied a lot, stayed up at night until wee hours of the morning, tried to pretend everything was normal while I was at school. I can't fail to mention my support system; my amazing classmates and professors who were beyond supportive of the situation. Today, looking back, I can say that I couldn't have done it without them. Yes, individuals with anxiety, and mental illness in general, need a lot of support; however, their caretakers need it just as much. Caretaking becomes their identity and they forget to take care of themselves. That is why they need to be reminded by other wonderful, understanding people to do so, or to even be taken care of by them to some extent. I am grateful for having such an amazing support system so I could finish school. Obtaining my master's degree in Mental Health Counseling has been my dream for too long for me to allow it to disintegrate before my eyes. I also have to thank my mother. As bad of a shape as she was in at the time, she never allowed me to sacrifice my education for her sake. The thought of missing out on a semester hurt her, and was not even in question. That is why she decided to sacrifice herself, and we worked as a team. This is how.

TEAMWORK

What I am going to write about now still sounds wild to me. I sometimes cannot believe that it was possible to do what we have done to achieve a goal. My goal. My goal that my family cherished as if it was their own. In the winter, Grandma had to leave because her tourist visa did not allow her to reside in the U.S. for longer than three months. At first we panicked, then tried to rationalize, then fantasized that it will be okay and mom will be fine when the semester starts. She wasn't. Just like she wasn't fine by the time the previous summer started, nor was she fine by the time summer ended and school started. So that winter, she picked herself up and went to college with me. Every single day. She brought a book, her phone, anything that could keep her occupied and entertained, including her lunch, and sat at the lounge on my classroom's floor, so we could both feel comfortable, and so I could attend classes carefree. My heart broke every time I had to drag her to school with me. Rushing her every time trains got delayed and I had to run to class, leaving her alone to sit in the hallway while I was in class, wondering whether chair was comfortable for her, and whether she was embarrassed to do that… I had lunch with her to keep her company every single day. And not once did I feel bad for not having fun with my friends; this was the least I could do for a woman who sacrificed days of her life for my dream. It helped tremendously that my friends were so understanding, and would sometimes come to hang out with us; those ended up even being fond memories at this time. Still, it occurred to me so many times to take mom's hand and go back home with her, to spare her everything that she was feeling at those moments. But it never occurred to me to leave for good; I know that leaving school was not an option – that would hurt us both even more.

My internship soon started, and luckily, it was at my previous job site, at LaGuardia Community College. I owe tremendous gratitude to my department over there. Specifically, to my supervisors and the director who knew the situation and offered themselves for mom to come and stay with us. She was spared the hallways and student lounges, and was able to stay inside of the office with us; she hung out at the break room, with me in the office when I had no clients, we were able to lunch together comfortably, and she felt different, happier.

Soon after, Grandma was able to come again, and I could leave mom at home. Anxiety about whether the phone will ring again as soon as I get a little further from my house was there, but at least she was comfortable at home, and that's what mattered to me. Grandma somehow always managed to distract her, and her panic attacks subsided by now; they would not happen as often. She continued work with her amazing therapist, and slowly started to get better. Of course, she was still attached to me and had questions about how I will go to work after graduation, etcetera; but that was something to think about later. At that time, my biggest concern was graduating, and then I would figure it out.

GRADUATION

The most emotional day ever. I have never felt so heavy with feelings; I laughed, I cried, I felt like I had so much weight to lift off myself. Pride, joy, sadness, relief, all came together in one big bubble that I carried with me throughout the day. And so did my parents – each of us carried their own. I remembered days of sacrifice that both mom and I contributed to my degree. I remembered tears of my classmates with whom I shared my story in Trauma class and sobbed loudly while responding to professor's question, "Where is mom now?" – "In the hallway." Every fear about whether I'll make it to this day went through my head, I was touched by the words of my classmates and professors who said that I've made it, and most of all, I was touched by tears of my parents who have never been prouder. After the ceremony, I put my cap on mom's head and congratulated her on making it – she was at least half deserving of me being on that stage that day. Had she thought of her own comfort, stayed in bed, and refused to do anything to help me out, I probably would not make it. Therefore, thank you, mom.

ANXIETY

Most of us experience some anxiety, almost on a daily basis. Job-related stress, family issues, arguments, annoyance with a rude stranger on the train, or simply feeling overwhelmed by the amount of responsibilities we have to complete every day. Anxiety, as it is, makes us worry about uncertainty of the future, or ruminate over what has been happening in the past. Neither of those is healthy, and both contribute to various symptoms that could become very debilitating. Just as each person's anxiety is unique to them, so are the symptoms. I've met and worked with many people with various forms of anxiety, and their symptoms greatly differed; sometimes, they were even opposite.

SYMPTOMS

Symptoms could be both physical and psychological. They could range from faulty cognitions - negative thoughts, and beliefs that convince us that we need to worry about what is going to happen a year from now, have an internal dialogue that runs through every possible scenario that could go wrong, and does not leave room for anything that could go right, to sweating, palpitations and belief that we are dying. From the voice that reminds us of every past mistake that we "shouldn't have made," that convinces us that we could've done something better, and presents a bunch of "what if" scenarios that continuously disrupt our peace, to tension headaches, numbness and tingling throughout your body, and tightness in chest.

Have you ever feared doing something wrong? Dying perhaps? Hurting somebody accidentally? Burning the house down because you did not trust yourself that you turned off the stove, so you had to check.... And check again, and again...? Have you worried about not being good enough? Making a terrible mistake at work that could cost you your job? Not being able to complete the coursework for the major that you've always dreamed of? Having your husband cheat on you? Not being liked by others? Feeling so stressed out to the point of being unable to complete any of the items on your "To Do List?" If your answer to any of these questions is "yes," you've experienced anxiety first hand.

What anxiety does is prevents us from doing what we

desire to do, and proves us right about being unable to do so. Let me explain: our worry that we cannot accomplish what we imagined, paralyzes us to the extent of really being unable to, or rather, believing that we are unable to do it, so we end up proving ourselves "right" – we cannot do it. Of course, then we become anxious about that, and that belief that we are not good enough, and unable to accomplish goals, makes us more stressed out, and forces our mind to create even more of illogical scenarios and self-defeating thoughts. We enter the vicious cycle which is very difficult to leave.

Thoughts multiply. Negative thoughts especially. If you wanted to make yourself anxious right now, you could do it very easily. Just imagine something that you fear could happen. I guarantee you that your mind could continue to go different ways, create more and more anxiety, more negative scenarios, more self-doubt, tens and tens of ways for everything you imagined going wrong. Try it, and just observe your thoughts, watch them multiply. And then recognize that the thought that started it all is just a thought that is a fantasy – everything will stop. All those fears, unsettling physical sensations, it will all be gone. Sounds impossible, right? But it is true. Why? Because you are the one in charge of your mind, it's simple as that. However, people who struggle with chronic anxiety, don't find it so easy to stop those thoughts because they actually do believe them. That is why some of the strategies that I will discuss in upcoming chapters could be helpful.

***

Physical symptoms are especially debilitating when it

comes to struggling with anxiety. Do you know that feeling in the pit of your stomach at the doctor's office? When you are in the waiting room and experiencing that anticipation anxiety, when you stomach churns, nausea begins, your palms sweat? Now imagine feeling that on more days than not, after every unpleasant thought or the situation. That is how people with anxiety feel. And these are only a few of the symptoms that are being reported. Heart palpitations, sweating, loss of appetite (or overeating in some cases), numbness in hands and arms, shallow breathing, hyperventilation, nausea, vomiting, lack of sleep, nightmares, tension headaches… are some of the symptoms that a person with anxiety could experience. *Often, anxiety is confused for another health problem, such as the heart attack, therefore, it is very important to exclude the possibility of another illness that could be contributing to the symptoms.*

Anxiety is very closely related to panic attacks, which are, in fact, expressions of severe anxiety. Panic attacks appear unexpected, and could happen when the person is seemingly feeling good. They come about due to a buildup of feelings and anxieties in general, and are usually very scary for the person who is experiencing them, especially for the first time. Panic attack activates the "Fight or Flight" response, and riles up physical sensations, while increasing vitals in the body. The person begins to sweat, hyperventilate, heartbeats per minute increase significantly, blood pressure rises, muscles tense and prepare to run, and adrenaline levels increase, in fact preparing the body for either fighting or flighting. These physical symptoms are usually accompanied by negative self-talk and catastrophizing, such as "I am going to die," "Something really bad is going to happen and I wouldn't be able to stop it," "I am going crazy," "I am out of control," etc. What is important to keep in mind is that one should not fight the panic attack for you cannot stop it. Panic attacks have to run their course that usually lasts about 30 minutes, with peek at about 10 minutes, after which they begin to subside. In my opinion, panic attacks are not a terrible thing; in fact, they help the person release all the bottled-up anxiety, and in a way, "reset." Don't be surprised if you are feeling like you want to sleep for days after having a panic attack; you've just fought with a bear, right? Or ran a marathon, in case of you athletes.

Physical and psychological symptoms are usually intertwined. Negative thoughts could stir up physical sensations, while physical sensations could also lead us to thinking that we're about to feel anxious - which, of course, we do end up feeling. In an example of my mom, for instance, allergies and asthma imitate symptoms of anxiety: shallow breathing that she experiences during high allergy seasons, is resembling shallow breathing during anxiety attacks, which triggers her thoughts that question whether she is getting anxious and why, which leads to actual anxiety. Again – vicious cycle.

Many clients report health-related worries and social anxiety, along with problems with being out in public or taking public transportation by themselves. Most of the identified concerns that lead to these avoidant behaviors are related to negative thoughts and fears about becoming very sick and dying, getting sick in the street and having no one around to help, or being judged or rejected by others in social settings. It is very difficult for those people to begin to believe otherwise, and to look at the situations as potentially having positive outcomes. Commonly, patients transfer worry to their children, spouses, parents, or even pets. They begin to worry about everything, no matter how insignificant it seemingly is – laundry not being done on time, dishes not washed, person on the train pushing them without saying "excuse me," child failing grade, friend not inviting them to the gathering, and often, these thoughts become obsessive and lead to greater anxiety.

TYPES OF ANXIETY

Anxiety varies from one person to the next, as well as from one diagnosis to the next. Not every anxiety is the same, as is the treatment. Symptoms, severity, causes, and frequency differ. I won't spend too much time talking about various anxiety disorders, as the purpose of this book is to help you handle the symptoms. I do, however, believe that the psychoeducation is the crucial part of treatment; therefore, I would like to briefly introduce you to a few of the most common anxiety disorders, and in that way, help you understand your symptoms better, and hopefully, learn about the fact that they are common and that you are not alone in feeling like this.

One common symptom that all anxiety disorders have is *avoidance*. And avoidance is the most problematic, as it turns our fears into monsters and makes them more so scarier. Which, of course, leads us to further avoidance, creating a vicious cycle that becomes difficult to escape. We will discuss facing your fears a little bit later, but I found it necessary to mention this as I introduce you to a few disorders that all have the element of avoidance. Separation Anxiety, for instance, creates avoidance of loneliness, being away from people you are close to, or that one person that you are particularly attached to. Selective Mutism creates fear of, and avoidance of, speaking in certain social situations. Social Anxiety prevents people from going out and being in social settings without undue feelings of anxiety, therefore, becoming debilitating and causing people to change their perception of being out, challenge their feelings of self-worth, and finally, making the decision to stay at home and avoid engaging with friends, family members, or romantic interests in social settings.

Specific Phobias are a fear of specific object or situation. Logically, the above mentioned will be avoided continuously and therefore, even the entertainment of the thought to engage in it and expose yourself to it, becomes anxiety provoking. You are probably familiar with, or could relate to, in some capacity, the fear of an animal (snakes and spiders are common), environment, such as heights, water, or storms, objects such as needles, means of transportation such as airplanes or elevators, or other, fear-inducing stimuli, that is specific to you. Another very common disorder, previously mentioned, is Social Anxiety Disorder, or as we more commonly call it, Social Phobia. People fear social gatherings that could lead to variety of anxiety producing situations such as feeling judged by others, looked at while one eats, being unable to start and/or hold a conversation, and finally, performing in front of a large group of people. Of course, people with this particular disorder avoid social gatherings, large crowds, and therefore, are creating even larger gap between them and others. Social interactions, therefore, become nearly impossible to take place.

Panic Disorder itself does not depend on other stimuli, therefore, avoidance is not a part of it, per say. However, person with Panic Disorder will fear having another attack, and therefore, try their best to avoid anything that could be perceived a trigger, or anything that they believe "caused" it the last time. Agoraphobia could include panic attacks, and also includes avoidance as it presents the fear of open spaces, long lines, train stations, outdoor crowds and noises. All the above trigger anxiety and panic, and therefore, people who suffer from Agoraphobia, tend to avoid leaving the house, leaving the house alone, or visiting triggering places.

Finally, Generalized Anxiety Disorder. Anxiety about anything and everything. About your past, present or future, about your decisions, about your family, about your health, about their health, about success at school, about relationships, job, and finances. Pretty much, everything you could think of and get anxious about. We've all experienced it to some extent, but might not have experienced impeded functioning because of it. This type of anxiety, just like others, leaves room for avoidance of triggers – responsibilities, independent decision-making, independent living, going to work, going home, engaging in a conversation, handling finances, completing homework, working on a project. Again, the more you avoid any of these activities, the scarier they become, and you become less likely to expose yourself to them and give them a try. Last, but not least, some people suffer from Substance/Medication Induced Anxiety, or Anxiety due to Another Condition. Therefore, it is always important to tell your doctor/therapist/psychiatrist, if you are on any medication or suffering from another condition that could contribute to symptoms of anxiety. For instance, thyroid conditions, asthma, endocrine problems, as well as some medications, such as Epi-Pen Injection.

ANXIETY FROM MY ANGLE

Before I introduce you to some of the strategies that could significantly improve your quality of life and make living with anxiety easier, it is important that I explain what is the reality that you should expect. Many people begin psychotherapy wanting to be completely anxiety free and never again experience the symptoms of it. I understand that desire, symptoms of anxiety are indeed terrifying. Unfortunately, I must disappoint you; anxiety cannot be cured. It is inborn to all of us and as a matter of fact, it could be very useful. Wait, don't throw the book away just yet, I will explain what I meant by that. Think of the cavemen, for instance. They didn't have anything that would inform them of impending danger, their bodies were their own tool. Their body served as an alarm that would inform them of the possible danger, just like it informs us when we are exposed to unpleasant situations such as the dentist visit or a job interview. In such way, our body prepares us for the successful completion of the upcoming tasks: in the example of the dentist, it increases our adrenaline, heart rate, and breathing, all of which would help us in pain management. Before the job interview, it helps us concentrate and wakes us up, and in that way assists us in feeling present and remain focused on that particular task. Do you now see how anxiety could be positive? It is inborn to all of us and we all carry it within, the only difference is that in some instances, it begins to get out of control and becomes too activated, even in situations in which it is not necessary.

Panic attacks, although very intense and scary, use as an exhaust for letting go of excess emotions. When our body becomes filled up with emotions, and we fail to process and take care of them in a timely manner, the body informs us of that and finds a way to regenerate itself. Your body is your best friend and the most knowledgeable tool about what it is that we need. Panic attacks, seemingly, occur out of nowhere, but think about how long have you been keeping those emotions for yourself, and when was the last time you stopped and decided to cleanse your body of them. It took your body a long time to collect all those emotions, and often, when we finally relax, it finds the right moment for the panic attack that will let go of everything that is negative.

This is why I would like that you start your treatment and battle with anxiety with an open mind and open heart, and view it not as your enemy, as hard as that could be. I know many people, including my mother, whose lives were improved by anxiety. How? In a way that anxiety forced them to take care of themselves, to take care of their mental and physical health, to make time for themselves and their needs daily, to allow themselves some mistakes – not everything has to be under control at all times. If you learn this and implement strategies that I will be writing about, unhealthy anxiety will no longer have a place in your life.

KNOW YOUR TRIGGERS

It is very important that you know what starts your anxiety. Did you notice that in certain situations, in certain company, and with certain thoughts, your anxiety increases? Observe this. Pay attention to what was happening in the moment you felt first symptoms – what were you thinking about, where were you, with whom, what were you doing at that moment. In that way, you will be able to recognize triggers that create feelings of anxiety within you, which will be of crucial importance for your treatment and yourselves. You will learn how to prepare for the trigger, how to handle it successfully, and finally, how to, over time, your trigger is no longer a trigger, but just another part of life with which you will deal as if any other.

EXPOSURE TO FEARS

One of the biggest problems for people with anxiety is that in their great fears, they begin to avoid everything that makes them feel uncomfortable, afraid or anything else that reminds them of the symptom of anxiety. You will meet people who avoid coming out of the house by themselves, those who avoid staying in it by themselves, who don't want to participate in activities that were once pleasurable, such as nights out, dancing, or driving a car. All that because at that one moment, as they were engaged in that activity, they felt anxiety and became convinced that it started it; it or one of its components. When we begin to avoid those activities, we start feeling guilty and begin stepping into the vicious cycle. Thoughts such as, "I can't do anything else," "I can't do this, I can't do that," "If I go there, I'll have a panic attack," and so on, start floating around our mind and really creating feelings of anxiety. We then confirm that anxiety created it, without the realization that, in fact, we contributed to it with our thoughts, and all over again, we avoid participating in it. What must happen is that we engage in that activity regardless of anxiety. When I say engage, and I don't mean fully and suddenly; I mean step by step. If you are used to long car rides of a few hours at the time, get into your car for five minutes only. If you enjoyed partying until the dawn, go for only one drink. When you confirm that this is nothing to be afraid of, that the territory is familiar to you, and at the same time, you repeat to yourself that the activity could be discontinued at any moment in which you feel uncomfortable, only then will you be able to slowly increase time spent engaging in it, and finally, with time, you will come back to where you used to be. Problem that many people have with it is that they feel guilty and underestimate themselves because, seemingly, they are learning to walk again. But that is not something to be embarrassed of. Imagine someone who had a surgery and who was bed-bound for a long time. Is it easy for that person to get up, move around normally, and participate in normal activities two days after the surgery? Of course it isn't. they need time to slowly come back to the rhythm. And we don't judge people in such positions, do we? We feel sympathetic towards them and understand what they went through. So why then do you judge yourself?

COPING STRATEGIES

AWARENESS/MINDFULNESS

Have you ever spent a day at the beach and dozed off under the sunlight? Have you noticed what the sunrays feel like on your skin, how the light breeze lightly brushes over your skin, making it more tolerable to spend more time laying under the sun? How your body is warming up, perspiring, how the sand is flying around under the breeze… Then your body begins to feel heavier, lazier, overall more relaxed… If you have, congratulations – you've spent some time being aware of your surroundings and mindful of your bodily sensations – both internal and external. If you are able to do this, either at the beach, or in a different environment, you are more than likely able to successfully become aware of your thought processes and physical sensations that accompany anxiety. When you start feeling anxious, try to focus on what that anxiety feels like (you can begin either by focusing on thoughts or physical sensations first); is your heart racing? Is your breathing shallow? Do you feel pressure on your chest? Numbness in your limbs? Or maybe a knot in your stomach? Whatever your sensations are, just notice them. Recognize them, name them, acknowledge them, and move on to the next one.

How about your thoughts? What is going through your head right now? Are you worrying about something that happened yesterday? Are you predicting what might happen a month from now and that is making you anxious? Did you start to panic about those unpleasant feelings that are stirring up in your body right now? Don't worry – it's only anxiety, and it is familiar to you. You know what it feels like, and you know that it cannot do you any harm. You also know that you are the one in control.

Let's try the opposite exercise now. If you are calm, reading this, and lounging in your favorite chair, you are not very likely to feel anxious (although, reading about anxiety might have made you so, which, don't worry, is not unlikely). If you are indeed calm, try to think of something that worries you: a bill you have to pay, difficult research paper with approaching deadline that you haven't even started on yet, your child's low grade in science class, a bloodwork result that was a little elevated, or whether your partner is still in love with you. Do you notice anything? A difference in your posture, breathing, heart rate? Did your palms begin to sweat, your mind to race? Is there a knot in your stomach? I bet your mind created the worst-case scenario too, am I right? Do you see how you created your own anxiety by only thinking *one negative thought*? How fascinating! Now, go ahead and calm yourself down by using the art of mindfulness/ awareness we have discussed just a minute ago.

Now imagine that same scenario that created your anxiety, only with the most positive outcome. You paid off that bill in full with no financial strain, you finished that paper on time, and got an A, your child was given extra credit, and received an A on his newest assignment which significantly boosted his science grade, your health is perfect and little elevation was due to the cold you suffered from recently, while the love of your life is still madly in love with you, and in fact, plans on surprising you with a romantic getaway next weekend. How do you feel now? Are you smiling? Are your breaths deep and your chest feels expanded and relieved off pressure? Your head is filled with positive energy and your tension headache at the base of your neck is gone? Your heart is beating hard but with excitement? Congratulations, you did it yourself! You just learned Lesson 1 in dealing with symptoms of anxiety. Here is how my long-term client did it:

"Self-awareness/mindfulness has helped me determine whether or not the situation I am dealing with is in my control or not. That determination then helps me to then put my feelings or thoughts in check, and then I can either proceed to process them or simply let go."

-Ann

AUTOMATIC THOUGHT RECORD (ATR)

ATR is, as I would say, a little pocket therapist. The principal of it is based on what I discussed previously –exploring all possible outcomes, and challenging your negative thoughts by exploring more positive scenarios. Its purpose is to bring you awareness about your thought processes, worries, and bodily sensations, and bring your anxiety down by asking you a series of questions that maybe a therapist would in psychotherapy session. Some of them include your worry, feared outcome, the best possible outcome, and of course, the scenario that is most likely to occur. By participating in this exercise, your anxiety will be reduced, and you will be able to think about your worries critically, and understand whether your worries are legitimate, exaggerated, or consist solely of fantasy and fear of anticipated events that may or may not occur. You could find copies on search engines such as Google, or in Cognitive Behavioral-based books. I highly recommend books by Dr. Judith Beck and Dr. Aaron Beck, who are the master minds behind Cognitive Behavioral Therapy and creators for worksheets such as the Automatic Thought Record.

BREATHING

Yes, we all breathe on a daily basis, many breaths a day, since the moment we are born, until the moment we die. But are we breathing the right way? Believe it or not, most of us are not. In fact, most of us find it difficult to breathe "the right way," because it's not something we are used to, and it doesn't come so naturally with every breath we take. I am talking about what we call, *belly breathing.* Belly breathing enables us to really get the full benefits of the breath, as it is the only way to breathe in enough oxygen, expand our presence, cleanse our mind, and relax our body. What we usually do is breathe into our lungs; however, that cuts off the full length of the breath in half – we allow it to reach our diaphragm, and send it right back out, so the abdominal area remains untouched by it. Allowing the full breath is crucial because many of us store our tension and stress in the abdominal area; in our stomachs and livers, more than any other organs. Therefore, do your little engines a favor and send through a few deep cleansing breaths, will you?

To achieve a full belly breath, we first need to be mindful of it. Let's do it together. Place your hands on your lower abdomen and sit comfortably with your posture upright. First exhale fully so you empty your body of everything that it doesn't need any longer. Then, take a full, deep breath through your nose. Feel the air in your nostrils, moving down towards your lungs through the esophagus, expanding your diaphragm, and finally reaching your belly that is now rising underneath your hands.

Hold it for a moment, and let it out completely through your mouth, noticing and remaining mindful of its movement starting from your belly that is now falling flat to your spine underneath your hands, up the abdominal organs, the diaphragm that is now contracting, up the esophagus, through the lungs that are contracting as well, and finally, out your slightly open mouth. Let's do this again. And again. With no rush. Do this about 8 times, and notice the difference in your body and mind. Life is not so bad anymore, is it?

MEDITATION

Meditation practice is probably one of the most interesting experiences and coping strategies for anxiety, and overall wellbeing. Meditation is not easy to get into, as it is unnatural to our body. Stillness, focus on our breathing alone, and observing our physical sensations and emotions without addressing them, is not something that we are used to, or do on a daily basis. This, however, *is* what should be our most natural state, but we allow outside factors to affect our physical and emotional states, and allow those feelings to take over. I am sure that many of you have tried meditating, but you either did not like it, it felt unnatural, or you just couldn't calm down those little needles that attacked your body and prompted you to move the moment you attempted remaining still.

When I first tried meditating, I, well, strongly disliked it. I somehow managed to achieve the opposite effect and get more anxious. Why? Probably because I tried to forcefully calm my body down, slow down my mind, and keep my body still, without really paying mind to what the guide was saying. I focused more on discomfort than on following directions and actually relaxing. It took me a couple of years to get into it and fall in love with meditation practice. Don't get scared, I did not actively try meditating for a couple of years daily, because I would have gotten into it way sooner, of course. It was just an idea floating in my head, and I admired those who were able to meditate for 20 minutes at the time. To me, it seemed mission impossible.

Until I found the meditation that I absolutely loved. I learned that the key ingredients were starting with short meditations, literally only a couple of minutes long, starting simple with only body scan and breathing, and ensuring that you are enjoying the guidance, including the voice of the person speaking to you (yes! It matters!). Of course, it is only natural to feel jittery at first, but what I suggest you do is embrace it instead of fighting it. Acknowledge those needles and urges to move, accept them, and continue on with what you're trying to do.

I downloaded a couple of meditation apps on my phone, and the one that worked best for me, and that I would highly recommend is *Calm. Calm* offers a variety of options, starting from guided meditations that address different feelings, help you feel gratitude, and share loving kindness, to sleep stories for adults and children alike. I started by using *Daily Calm* option called *"7 Days of Calm." "7 Days of Calm"* was just that – guided meditations of approximately 7 minutes long, starting from scratch, and really teaching you what meditation is. Meditations are short enough to help jittery beginners remain present and successfully complete practice, but long enough for you to reap its benefits. Keep in mind that the length of meditation does not matter – *Calm* offers sessions only 2 or 3 minutes long, and sometimes, when I need a quick reminder to be mindful, they will do the job. As for *"7 Days of Calm,"* it really helped me learn how to remain in the moment, run the body scan, focus on my breathing, and most of all, regulate my emotions, and help myself think about my reactions before I execute them. As I continued to practice meditation daily, I found myself eager to get home from work to do another daily session; I started to build a habit. For those of you who are competitive, goal-oriented souls,

Calm offers a calendar that helps you keep track of your sessions. One of my motivations was keeping a meditative streak, and hoping to achieve a 21-day streak that will help me build a habit, and move on to the next goal – a 90-day streak after which you are able to say that your habit is now a lifestyle – scientifically proven (check out 21/90 rule). Another feature that I found rewarding was a nice quote and a virtual tap on the back in the form of "Good job!" or "You're amazing!" that the app would give me at the end of each session.

I got comfortable with meditating fairly quickly, and what I learned along the way was that I was now more able to explore further and actually enjoy meditation and focus on it no matter the voice of the guide, no matter the accent, no matter the content. I was *present*. After some time, I broke my streak due to travel, but I knew that I will not stop meditating for good if I skipped a day. My body will remind me to do it, and I will want to feel the benefits of meditation again. Meditation, in fact, became my *lifestyle*. Note: I did not even get to the 90-day mark yet, I was around day 50, and I still came back to it without any problems.

I utilize meditation practice in my work with clients as well. I encourage them to practice mindfulness, breathing techniques, and meditation on their own. Many of them shared benefits that I am experiencing as well. Only some of the benefits include increased focus and concentration. When meditating regularly, we clear our minds, are more in tune with our thoughts, feelings, and physical sensations, and therefore, able to clear the clutter of our minds, with that increasing our ability to retain information, focus on the present moment, concentrate on the task, and recall information without clouded mind. Changed reactivity to outside factors is one of the benefits I recognize in myself the most, and appreciate the most, as it was the most debilitating problem of mine. Remember that exercise from earlier in the book where I talked about making yourself anxious by a single negative thought? Meditation will teach you to recognize that thought, allow it to process in your mind, acknowledge it, explore your feelings and physical sensations connected to it, and let it go. It is as simple as that once you realize that thoughts and feelings are not permanent. They are only temporary visitors in our daily lives, and *cannot harm us.* Thoughts are only thoughts and you are in control of them.

A big part of meditation is *mindfulness.* Mindfulness is crucial in treatment of anxiety, particularly to help you get in tune with your own thoughts, feelings and bodily sensations that occur as a result. If you are experiencing any debilitating thoughts, let's say, about your upcoming doctor's appointment; there are two directions in which this could go. First, and most probable one if you are not mindful, is the worst-case scenario. You thought about visiting the doctor, and your mind is now being creative and taking you all kinds of different places – you will be afraid, the wait time at the office will be long, you hate getting injections and he may prescribe one, then he'll run different tests that will probably be uncomfortable, and finally give you results about having a life-threatening disease. Do you see how far you can get with your imaginary scenarios? Creative, right? This, of course, will lead to variety of unpleasant symptoms of anxiety.

Now, what would happen if we became mindful of this cycle, if we "caught" our own thoughts and challenged them as soon as they are born in our mind? What if we acknowledged the thought and said, "I worry about the outcome of this doctor's appointment," but then further explored possible outcomes without going straight to the most negative one? I would suggest acknowledging everything that you worry about; the wait time, fear of needles, uncomfortable testing, the worst possible outcome. But then, I suggest you challenge that, and question yourself in the opposite manner – How do you know the wait time will be long? Is it necessary for the doctor to prescribe an injection? Are you really terminally ill, what facts support this fear? After running through these questions, you'll notice that your answers are completely different than your fears; in fact, your anxiety may seem a little silly now. Pay attention to your anxiety levels as the possible outcomes in your head are more positive; less anxiety, right? I'll give you're the magic word for this part as well – *facts*. Always challenge yourself with actual facts.

- What proves to me that the wait time in the office will be long?
  » Nothing, I can't know that ahead.
- How do I know that the doctor will prescribe an injection?
  » I don't, it is only my fear that he may, but I can't know for sure.
- What are the signs that I am terminally ill?
  » There are none, I am feeling pretty good and going to the doctor for an annual visit.

See what I did here? *Facts*. Now, if you are stubborn like

my mother was when she was anxious for instance (and anxiety will make you stubborn), you, or rather, your mind, will challenge even these answers, and find another "but" in them. What do you do in that case? Continue the process by exploring the more acceptable, realistic outcome, and ways to cope with it. For instance, if the wait is long, how can I make it productive? No, not by worrying about what will happen inside of the office when the doctor calls your name, and definitely not by looking at your watch and counting minutes. Remember, we are talking about mindfulness here, *remain in the present moment*. You may bring a book to read, you may meditate in the waiting room, you may engage in a conversation with a nice elderly lady sitting next to you, you can read office magazines, or even bring a project, homework, or documentation to work on. Make productive use of the time. Now, check in with your anxiety. Wait time is actually not so bad if used right, huh?

Now, how about that injection, those uncomfortable tests? What is the worst that could happen? Ok, they may run a few tests, touch you with cold gloves, plug you onto an EKG machine – nobody likes that. But, is it life-threatening? Your fear of discomfort is creating your anxiety here, so why don't we try to look at it from a different perspective – if you run those tests, you will know how you're doing, and either be relieved that everything is perfect, or be able to help yourself if something is in fact wrong. In both scenarios – good thing you've done it!

Every meditation practice will teach you the most important thing – coming back to your *breath*. It is a go-to in meditation practice, but also in mindfulness in general. If you notice your mind racing, your attention getting lost in the whirlwind of thoughts, and you notice rising physical sensations – come back to your breath. Simply remind yourself to slow down and focus only on the sensations of your breathing. Take full, deep belly breaths as described in the previous section, and you will notice that your mind and body are quieting down, and that your anxiety is probably not as elevated as it was just a few moments ago.

JOURNALING

Another helpful strategy is *journaling*. You may wonder what writing down may do for you and your anxiety, how will it help? It's very simple. Think about all those thoughts, worries, and ideas that are multiplying in your head. Think about how present and immediate they are, how they are impacting your mood, wellbeing, and relationships with others. How many times did you snap at somebody because you felt anxious and overwhelmed? How many chores were left undone because you could not bring yourself to do another one because everything is always on you and that gets you frustrated? How many nights did you spend rolling around in bed not being able to fall asleep because of your anxiety, and how many nights did it wake you up in the middle of the night when you had to be at work early in the morning?

If you were able to answer any of the above affirmatively, you may want to consider journaling. Imagine all those thoughts that are so overwhelming written down and magically put away in a box. A box that is only yours, and that will keep your worries for you, so you don't have to keep them until the morning. You will lock them away, and could pick them back up in the morning, if you wish. Otherwise, they will wait for you there if you ever want them back; you know, to analyze them a bit more. Get yourself a pretty notebook, anything that you connect with, or even use a regular blank piece of paper - anything works! This is great to do before you go to bed, so you can sleep peacefully and know that everything you are thinking about is waiting for you and you will not forget to pay attention to it. Of course, you can do it at any time of the day; you can journal like a teenager, daily, talking about how your day went, but also journal only at times of heightened emotions, particularly stress as it relates to anger or anxiety.

When you journal due to stress, PLEASE feel free to LET GO. Don't pay attention to punctuation, ways to put sentences together, whether it makes sense or not… It doesn't have to, it's only *yours*. You are not writing this to publish it or have anybody read it, you are writing it to release emotions and to feel lighter. Allow yourself to write down anything that comes to mind. Free up some of the darkest things you wanted to say to somebody, but knew better, some of the most intense emotions that you are ashamed to speak about. Write them all down. I promise you, you will feel liberated. Once you write it all down, close that notebook and feel in control. Take a moment to reflect on having emptied your head, but still be in ownership of your thoughts and feelings – only put away and categorized in the little box (you can also lock that notebook in a little box, so it can be even more so symbolic). After that, you will be able to free yourself from those emotions, and as you vented out, you may be able to now think clearly about what has happened and what you're actually feeling. Once you sleep on it, you may notice that all those emotions that created a confusing salad in your head could probably be defined as only one emotion, and you will know how to deal with it. What do I mean by this? When you feel anxious, do you ever get confused about what is it that you are actually feeling? You feel angry, upset, sad, overwhelmed, stressed out, guilty, you may be yelling and crying… But once you shed all of that, what remains? Hurt? Burden that has been placed on you and you don't know what to do with it? Tired? You name it, it could be it. But the only way to do something about it is define it, and your journal will help you get to that point.

One of my clients who've made tremendous success in therapy throughout the period of only a year and a half (a year and a half before he started to feel significantly better, although the journey towards his improvement was paved by successes after only a few months), uses journal writing as a strategy for coping not only with anxiety, but with other emotions such as anger and symptoms of depression. Here is what he said:

"Writing helps a lot because of the freedom you feel.
You can write about anything and everything.
How you are feeling, what's bothering you,
and even random thoughts you have.
No matter how simple, writing always helps.
Plus, remember the best writers are the ones who
suffered from depression and even anxiety."

–Joshua Mercado

LISTS

This leads me to different kinds of lists. Lists are very helpful… well, for everything. You've all heard of TO DO Lists, Shopping Lists, Guest Lists; but there are other kinds of lists that are just as, if not more useful, and that I call Worry Lists. Like journals, these lists take care of your emotions. However, they are not quite the same. You can use worry lists whenever you want; however, I usually recommend them to clients who feel anxious at night, who get woken up by anxiety, or find it difficult to fall asleep because they feel overwhelmed by all the things they have to do the next day, who worry about forgetting to complete the task in the morning, or that research paper that you have a great idea about, but may forget it until the next day. Worry Lists are amazing for that.

If you sit down before going to bed, explore what's going on in your mind in that moment, understand what is preventing you from relaxing, and finally write bullet points of all those things, miracle may happen. You may be able to notice how anxiety is slowly diminishing because you are no longer stressed out about forgetting to do something, or about that amazing research paper idea. What I do want to suggest though (and this is what is making Worry Lists different from TO DO Lists), is that you literally write down your *worry*. To write down, "I worry about how I will do on this presentation on Monday," "I worry about waking up late in the morning," "I worry about forgetting this great idea for my paper," and any thoughts that might be accompanying those current worries. You will see how many of them will be there in the morning. Most likely none because you've emptied those thoughts and feelings from your head, placed them on paper, and therefore, freed yourself from their negativity, and prevented them from multiplying in your head.

Another use for Worry Lists is to remind you (watch this wittiness) – to worry! Sometimes, when you absolutely need to be productive – in school, at work, writing a paper, focusing on a meeting, etc., your worries decide to come around and mingle in your head, only to prevent you from concentrating and completing your task successfully. In that case, I suggest you take a minute to write down your worries on a piece of paper, and leave it aside. Symbolically tell the paper to keep your worries for you until you finish the task, and that you will then come back for them. And make sure you do! You can also make a worry box that you can decorate as you wish, and use it as storage for all your worries (I particularly recommend this for young children). As I might have mentioned before, we are sometimes afraid to let go of our anxiety and worries, which then makes us cling on to them as if we're holding on for dear life! When you make a list, you are not completely pushing them away or ignoring them, rather, you are just postponing worrying. Once you go back to that paper, or open the box, and reread your worries, you will then tackle them one by one. Of course, if they are still there given that many of them could have been related to what you were doing a few minutes ago, or, your completed task may put you in a mood good enough that you will no longer feel the need to worry, as you will be feeling so much happier, relieved and positive.

Another list that we already mentioned and that is not a Guest List, is a TO DO list. We are all familiar with them, but do we actually think about their value other than reminding us about things that we have to get done? Imagine having to memorize every little task you have to do; every phone call, memo at work, every e-mail, the time of every upcoming meeting… A lot, right? And by "a lot" I mean stressful. And it is, terribly. That's why you should maximize utilizing those lists, and writing down every nitty gritty detail of the things you have to do. I scribble, cross over, check off, add, you name it! And it feels great! I always end up feeling accomplished, and every check mark next to an accomplished item is another sigh of relief. I write every single phone call, upcoming conversation, question to ask, present to buy, note to write, e-mail to compose – literally everything. And guess what, if I don't finish accomplishing everything that's on my list, I am at least able to see that I worked on some of those items and that I have still made progress.

The important thing is *prioritizing*. My TO DO List currently is a part of my planner (will get into that in a minute). It is divided into *top priority*, *priority*, and *errands*, but also into two separate sections – Work To Do List and Personal To Do List. And I use those sections as well, which helps me relieve some anxiety about tasks that I don't get to accomplish as planned. Those are usually the tasks that could be done tomorrow or a week from now, and have no urgency to them. Another great thing is that my TO DO List is weekly, and therefore, I feel ok about postponing some things until tomorrow. And worse comes to worst, I let them bleed over into the next week; at least those that are not too important, and often could, but don't have to get done. Here is how lists help Ann:

"I use To Do Lists or check lists when I know I have a busy week coming up. That helps me stay focused and get each task done one at a time. It helps to "break down" the bigger picture so I am not so overwhelmed."

–Ann

Now that I mentioned the planner, let that be my next idea for diminishing your anxiety. Planners are great. They really help you plan out your day, schedule events, check in on your availability, and allow you to effectively plan your life. Personally, I use my planner to schedule clients, mark events, highlight important dates, schedule socialization events with my friends, vacation time, days off, etc. Don't be afraid to get creative! I ordered so many cool stickers from Amazon, and utilize them on a daily basis. They make your planner not only look prettier, but help you see things that you look forward to doing stand out in a cute and colorful way. I also use color pens for different activities, and even to differentiate between clients at my various job locations – each location has its own color!

Having everything in one place definitely helps you stay

on track with various activities, and understand the balance between your work and play time. This may help you gain insight into some changes you might want to make to your life in order to improve different areas, or make it healthier. I suggest to my clients to utilize planners as a time management strategy, and really understand the value of the minute, and be realistic about what they want to accomplish throughout the day, and whether that is really possible.

When I worked at LaGuardia, I held a group focusing on Time Management and Study Strategies. One of the things we did was complete weekly time tables with ALL activities, including personal hygiene. Yes, personal hygiene! Again, understanding the value of a minute! Some of us take 10 minutes in the bathroom in the morning, others need 30. That would determine our wake-up time, commute to wherever we need to get, left over time to have breakfast, coffee, or find an outfit (which I, by the way, recommend finding the night before, but that's a whole different topic). For that particular reason, I asked students to input all their activities, travel time, exercise time, dinner-making, time to complete homework, time to complete parts of research papers, to read, make phone calls, go to work, spend time with friends and family, etc. This will allow you to really see how you can make the best of your time. Remember to be generous and realistic – leave a few extra minutes with transportation or homework, for instance. Trains get delayed, there is traffic on the roads, buses break down. Homework may take longer than expected because you may be tired, feel ill, have unexpected visitors, or be unclear on some questions that you may have to brush up in your textbook. But even after implementing that generosity approach, I'm sure that you will be able to find some free time for yourself, or to turn already booked time into double productivity. How, you may wonder? Let's get into that a bit more.

If we are on the train, for instance, what do we do? Usually stress out about possibly running late, but that is not the most productive thing to do, is it? Instead, take a look at your TO DO List and whatever you had planned for the day so far, and see what you can complete while commuting. Maybe you can finish some readings for the next day, maybe respond to some e-mails through your smart phone, possibly meditate, call a friend, schedule an upcoming doctor's appointment, maybe even write out an outline for your term paper, or if you're a therapist, send messages to clients to schedule their appointments. Maybe you can read a book for fun that you didn't get a chance to read and you've been wanting to, reach out to relatives and friends, or even have your morning coffee while reading the news! All is allowed and all of the above are time consuming tasks that could be completed on the train, and leave some free time for you when you get home to relax. I know, I know, you forgot what relaxation means.

Now that you learned how to combine TO DO Lists and planners, let's talk about finding what works for you. Everybody's style is different, and everybody is (dis)organized differently. Now, don't take my (dis) as disrespect, it's actually a cool, unique style that I've been admiring in people until this day. Some of us function best when everything is clear, neat, color-coded, and spelled fully and correctly. Others, however, function most effectively when their pages are messy, words crossed over, scribbled around randomly, and mostly written out as acronyms. Although I belong to the first group of people mentioned in this paragraph, I still somehow managed to dive into the mystical worlds of messy writing to be used as a memory device. You've guessed right – in college, when there was no time to be neat and highlight while words disappeared from the blackboard quicker than they were written. So, if you wish to cross over, tear, rip, scribble, please feel free to do so, as long as it helps you stay on track and reduces your stress.

To continue about what works for you, I have been on a hunt for a functional planner that matched my needs for, pretty much, years. As a student, I had it a little easier, as my planner consisted of important dates, and my TO DO List was divided into dates according to deadliness. As I became a professional and an official adult, my needs for a planner greatly changed. I needed space to schedule clients, to write important dates, plan social events, plan workshops, include my personal errands, and make quick notes as necessary. Needless to say, some planners that I tried turned out to be very messy once I've written down everything that needed to be written down – and somehow, that worked too, as I was able to more easily recall information I needed to remember. Interesting what our mind does, right? After years-long search, I finally heard of the *Passion Planner*. *Passion Planner* is awesome as it has all in one! TO DO Lists, as mentioned above, space for notes/drawings/your own quotes, hourly and weekly schedules, as well as a monthly calendar, blank pages to be used at your own creativity, gridded pages because why not? And the coolest of all, ways to write down your short and long term goals, break them down into smaller steps, and my favorite - weekly motivational quotes. To top it all off, planner itself looks very pretty and professional, and fits into smaller purses, ladies! *Passion Planner* really spreads fast by the word of mouth, so my friends and I love it, while I also recommended it to some of my clients who fell in love with it as well, and made great use of it.

Last, but certainly not the least of my lists (well, this was an interesting statement), are *pros/cons*. These lists could be used for any decision making or doubts you may be experiencing. I recommend using these lists to my clients in sessions, because they give us some sought after clarity, and both them and I are able to gain insight into their values, thought processes, and how those impact, or could potentially impact, their lives in the future. Some of the most popular instances of utilizing these lists are career-related decisions, and believe it or not, relationships. Who would've thought that we could put our romantic partners on a piece of paper and tear them apart into pieces to be explored? I'm sure it does not sound too nice when I say it that way, but believe me, it's an eye opener. What I mean by that is that you can clearly see every aspect of your decision in question clearly on paper, and you'll be able to measure its value. When you are solely thinking about it, it gets jumbled up in your head, and creates anxiety. This way, all your thoughts, both positive and negative, go into the two columns, and leave no room for anxious feelings.

Let me correct myself here for a second; when I say positive and negative thoughts, I am going to stop myself, ask you to rewind and remember something – there are no positives and negatives in the typical expectation of the *pros/cons* list – there are only *values*. And values are different for everybody. What you may find amazing or at least tolerable, I, or somebody else, may find it completely unacceptable and a deal breaker. It all depends from one person to the next, from their needs and expectations of their job, relationship, vacation, or whatever else you are deciding on. A pair of shoes, I don't know. Yes, you can definitely utilize those lists for purchasing shoes and being indecisive – I'm serious. Don't take yourself too seriously, work on yourself, get to know the person you are deep down, and have fun while doing that, learning and exploring. Everything that I talked about in this book so far, and everything that is coming up, is really about getting to know yourself, understanding your basic needs and expectations, your potentials, your comfort zones, goals, fears, and emotions. There is nothing more beautiful than doing that. And in many ways, I do believe that anxiety is actually an ice breaker, and a catharsis that leads you towards the path to self-exploration. Embark on that journey, and get to know the real you!

YOUR COGNITIONS

Have you ever wondered where beliefs and opinions about yourself, your personality, needs, appearance, come from? Are they all solely based off of your own feelings, or are they learned? Have you had a parent who constantly told you something about yourself that you possibly didn't agree with, but started to believe in because it was repeated to you so much? Did a neighboring child ever call you stupid to the point where the next time you got a grade lower than an A on a class paper, began to wonder whether he was right? If your mother constantly told you that you're the same as your father, although you didn't think so, your next excuse for cursing when you get angry became, "Well, I took after my father."

I'm sure you can think of plenty of examples such as this one, and maybe challenge what I wrote by saying, "but I am really like that." Think again. *Really* think about the first time you thought that about yourself; what was the situation, who was there, what did they say, why did you believe it, and how did the thought even occur to you? I am fairly certain that you were not the one who said it first. Somebody just said it at the vulnerable time, when you were feeling doubtful enough to believe it. And if they continued to say it, and if it continued to cross your mind every time you felt like a failure, twenty years later, it begins to describe who you are.

In sessions with clients, I am often faced with false, or troubling, core beliefs. Many clients are very much set in their ways, and even have difficulty believing that therapy may help them change those beliefs. "I can't," "I could if I only wasn't _______," "I'm like that and I can't change," are only some of the self-sabotaging sentences I hear almost on a daily basis. And believe it or not, those are some of my favorite statements, because they motivate me to challenge my clients' thought processes, and to help them turn their negative internal dialogue into a positive one. I challenge the belief and ask them to provide facts. It's not difficult to guess that often times, they have no facts to report, and if they do, they happen to be coincidental and really cannot describe their personality, because guess what? Even if one situation supports them, there are ten others to beat them. My goal for all of you who have negative/false core beliefs, is to turn them into positive ones. But first things first – you need to find out where they come from, and whether they are truly *yours*. This process of learning and exploration, going back through the time machine, and having epiphanies, may be too big of a bite for you to chew on your own – that's why therapy exists. However, this doesn't mean that you cannot do at least something on your own.

Whenever you give up on something you really want, whenever you say, "I can't," and doubt that you can accomplish your dream, ask yourself for *proofs*. Do you have the skills? Do you have the ability? Do you have the time? Challenge your thoughts by questioning whether there are facts that show otherwise, and if there are, how can you overcome them? As I have said many times over throughout this book, and as I say it dozens of times throughout the day in my work with clients – **thoughts are very powerful**. They can make or break you. That's why, take charge, challenge them, turn your "can'ts" into "cans," and try! Take a task that you believe you could never accomplish, and start small. If you were convinced that you could never solve a complicated math problem – try it! If you thought you could not draw to save your life – try it! If you believed that you could never get fit – go running on 7 consecutive mornings and check again! If, however, you really cannot solve a complicated math problem, or are not the most talented artist, does that mean that you are worthless, stupid, and lack talent in general? On the contrary – it means that you should explore your other talents and find what you are good at. Sometimes, our troubles lie in unfulfilling choices that we are making. If you are miserable at your job, question why? If you are forcing yourself to engage in a hobby only because your friend did, or because your mom wants to live vicariously through you, but you are genuinely not good at it – why not try something that you enjoy instead of believing that you are stupid? Bottom line is, *your beliefs are not always true*, and you should never do something only because you believe that that is the right thing to do. *Find yourself.*

There is a beautiful quote by Albert Einstein that reads:

"Everybody is genius. But if you judge a fish by its ability to climb a tree, it will live its whole life believing that it is stupid." – Albert Einsten

CIRCLE OF CONTROL

Anxiety is tightly connected to the feeling of control – if we suspect that we don't have enough of it, we begin to panic. That is why it is important to understand that we can't always keep everything under control and that that is very difficult to achieve, given that we are only human beings who, unfortunately, cannot control their environment a hundred percent and at all times. One of the exercises that helps this knowledge and which will, paradoxically, help you to feel more in control, is the exercise that we call Circle of Control. Draw two circles on a piece of paper, one within the other. On the inside of the bigger circle, in the smaller circle, write down all the things that you can control. What belongs to that list are your own emotions, choices, lifestyle, eating habits, work that you do, way in which you relate to others, what time do you go to sleep, when do you travel, etc. When you are done, start filling in the larger circle and in it write down all those things that are outside of your control. For instance, others' emotions and reactions, traffic, bus timetables, wars in the world, lives of your loved ones, behaviors of people on the street... This exercise could be used for a specific problem in your life and focused on a specific situation. It will help you gain a realistic perspective of the situation and dedicate yourself to those things in the smaller circle – things that you can control and for which you could plan steps towards resolution. Big circle is the big picture that is out of your reach. And why stress over something that is out of your reach and what you cannot influence? This is much harder to do without writing it down, because often, in the midst of emotions, we cannot clearly think about what we indeed can control and with that, we serve ourselves big bites unrealistically, while thinking that we can influence something that we really can't. Putting our control on paper, we have an overview of everything that is happening to us, and with that – control at least over that.

PRAYER

Whether you are religious or spiritual, atheist or agnostic, I'm sure there is something that you believe in. It has been research proven (yes, you can look it up!) that prayer lessens anxiety, provides a soothing feeling of comfort, and allows you a piece of mind knowing that somebody or something else is with you on this journey. It is important not to pray only when you need something; pray daily, give gratitude. Every morning, at night before going to bed, or randomly throughout the day when you feel the need, thank your chosen Higher Power for being there for you, and give gratitude for what you already have; health, love, food on your table, roof over your head, family, good job, ability to read and write, a beautiful child… even ability to afford that expensive piece of furniture or electronics! It all counts! The point is, don't take anything for granted, and don't only connect to your Higher Power when you feel like things are not going so well.

Why prayer works? For one, you feel like you're never alone. You can turn to your chosen Higher Power whenever you feel the need to – it doesn't even have to be a full on, on-your-knees prayer. It can just be a brief check-in-recital in your head; anywhere you are. And yes, it counts. As long as you really believe in that connection, the ability of your H.P. to help you, and you feel that comfort and soothing feeling that comes with letting go of some control, you're doing just fine. We're often having difficulty relinquishing our need for control, which is, for the most part, what causes our anxious feelings. During prayer, try to hand that control over to the H.P., at least for a brief few minutes, and notice the difference. Imagine that somebody who has the power to help you and solve all your problems is listening very carefully and taking notes on the other side. Imagine that they will help you when the time is right for you to receive help, and once you have experienced what you needed, and learned lessons that you are supposed to learn. Believe in that with all your heart, and notice the difference in your mind and body; do you feel calmer? Taken care of? Understood? Better able to sleep? I'm sensing some hesitation in my readers now, but I assure you that, if you keep practicing prayer daily, you will see its longer-term benefits. Feeling consistent connection with the H.P. is going to build a sense of confidence with you, and with that, belief that you can overcome anything that you're presented with.

I learned about prayer by my favorite great-Granny, who passed away in 2002, when I was about 12 years old. Granny pretty much raised me, since she lived with us and babysat me while my parents were at work. This is the person that I had the greatest connection with, the most beautiful conversations, and with whom I created the most amazing memories. Since I was a small child, she taught me how to pray every night; sometimes we did together, and those were truly wonderful moments, that I believe, greatly contributed to an even stronger connection between us since we connected on a much more intimate spiritual level. Granny always taught me to thank God for everything I have (if you are not Christian, again, choose your own H.P.), and to recite a small universal prayer before going to sleep. Since then, I do it every night. I chose my own way of praying, my own way of connecting, and a small spiel that is only my own and that I recite as I pass by my mother's tiny altar created to hold all the icons of the saints that she feels have helped her throughout her life, particularly illness. This helps me to go to sleep calmer, and knowing that He will be there for me no matter what, gives me strength to overcome my troubles – which is not such a bad deal, right?

I feel the need to briefly talk about Granny who helps me as well. Sometimes, when I am going through a difficult time, or when I just miss her more so than usual, I pray to her as well. I talk to her, knowing that she is listening to me, and will stand up for me and show me the right path, as she always did. Her wisdom, life experiences, and great understanding of me, have always yielded the best results; and I truly believe that she is by my side always, although not physically with me. This provides me with a sense of comfort that she used to induce in me by applying light pressure to the both sides of my hand, around my palm, holding my much smaller hand in her chubby, soft one. Do you have a person like that? Somebody who has called you the funniest, most unique pet name that you could barely pronounce and it made you giggle, but made you feel the most loved? Pray to that person, don't let that connection ever disappear. And if that person is still alive, well – lucky you.

PETS

Yay! I'm sure that was everyone's reaction because you know what's coming. Yes, pets are amazing for anxiety! Your fuzzy or feathery best friend can totally assist you in feeling better and reduce your symptoms of anxiety in such a fun and cuddly way! Whether you have a dog, a cat, a bird, or a fish, they can all do it in various wonderful ways. Most people with anxiety experience the need to do something with their hands – remaining calm is not an option. Some use stress balls, others are punching bags at the gym, some are doodling on a piece of paper, while most of us are clicking back and forth from Facebook to Instagram because, you know, a lot could happen in twenty seconds, and God forbid we miss it. That's when pets come in handy, and we looove cuddling with them! Petting soft fur/hair of a pet, or just holding one in your hand (like I do my parakeet buddy Kica), calms you down, and produces soothing feeling, allowing you to focus on the present moment. Animals also have a lot of positive energy, and are able to transmit it to you, while collecting any of your negative, anxious ones. Their unconditional love and connection you feel with them, is even more so important than their soft outfit.

I remember calling my puppy that I had as a child my best friend, as she really was one. Every time I was sad, I would hide behind the house in the backyard, sit down on a grass with her, cuddle and tell her about my day. Sometimes I would cry, and I will never forget the sad, comforting eyes that she looked straight into mine with. She would stay there for as long as I needed her, and I would always feel better. Today, I have Kica, who is a real human being. Kica I often see as my brother, as he really is a part of our family. He is always there to lighten the mood in the house, and to make us all laugh. As every other animal, he also feels when something is wrong, and would come to comfort us on his own. Whenever mom is experiencing any anxiety, he is on her shoulder, silently chirping. Whenever I am stressed out, he is on my hand, sending kisses back to me, and calling my name repeatedly. Often, you could find him in my hair, pulling the strains of hair out of my bun, which also helps me feel better as it feels like a little massage.

Basically, anything that animals do can be soothing in one way or another. Even fish are great companions and could even assist with meditation. My fish Sigmund Fica, is a colorful beta for whom I decorated a bowl with very soothing plants, treasure chests, and stones. Observing his peaceful floating and swimming, even eating, is very comforting, brings you back to the present moment, and almost forces you to focus on him as his mesmerizing colors and fins move across the depths of the bowl. So, if you don't have a fuzzy or a feathery friend that you can take into your hands and cuddle with, do not despair – your fish will be a good enough companion. The beauty of animals is also that you never feel alone. Their presence in the home makes a difference, and especially helps those who have anxiety about being alone in the home. Talking to animals, cuddling with them, and listening to their chirping, barking or meowing, for sure helps remind you that you have somebody by your side.

Whether you've heard of it or not, pets are often used in psychotherapeutic treatment (go look it up!), and their effectiveness has been proven to be very successful. Some of the most popular ones are therapy dogs (particularly Labradors), bunnies, and cats, especially breeds that are calm like the above-mentioned Labs, for instance. Petting animals, talking to them, and confiding in them is very therapeutic, as it stimulates all the senses whose soothing results in reduction of symptoms of anxiety. If you haven't already done so, get yourself a furry, fuzzy, feathery, or swimming friend, and embrace his help on your journey to becoming anxiety-free.

BE JUDGEMENT-FREE

Being judgement-free in our relationships with others is a virtue and a beautiful quality that we like to practice. We like to be there for others, accept them as they are, and ensure that they are feeling good and can be their real selves in front of us. These are all wonderful things that make us nice human beings. But how much of this are we doing for ourselves? How often do we stop to think whether we are judging ourselves? Are we being compassionate to ourselves? I'm sure that many of you will be unable to remember the last time you felt compassionate towards yourself, and you will probably find an excuse along the lines of "I don't have the time for that," or worse, "I don't deserve it." Wrong and Wrong. EVERYONE DESERVES IT. And if you can be so wonderful to others, why can't you be to yourself?

Understanding your own feelings, giving yourself the right to experience them and validate them, hugging yourself and saying, "I know you are going through a lot," may sound crazy, but it's truly what you need. By judging your own feelings, you are punishing yourself for something you are not at fault about. Think about how many times you've thought of somebody who hurt you and made up an excuse for them? Meaning, you showed compassion and empathy to that person. But what about yourself? Do you matter?

Another form of judgement of self that I often face in my work with clients, is that of judging oneself whenever one is not doing perfectly. What do I mean by that? With anxiety specifically, once clients get a hold of coping strategies, their anxiety symptoms begin to reduce due to their ability to cope with them in an effective way. However, anxiety doesn't just disappear – its symptoms improve and worsen as days go by. None of it means that you're a failure or incapable of coping with them. What it means instead is that you are going through motions, and it's important to continue to work hard on getting better, and *not falling* the moment something goes not as planned. Most of the clients that I have had the pleasure of working with, judge themselves and report feeling like a failure when they can't effectively reduce their anxiety on some days. Think of it this way; even if you never had anxiety, was your mood exactly the same every day? Did you feel happy all the time and never woke up feeling "off?" Of course you were not. And for no reason on many days, I'm sure. You just "got up on the wrong foot," as we say. Think of babies too, they're a perfect example. Babies have no anxiety, they have no real-life problems to be fussy about, yet they are! They have some bad, some good days, some days they decide to cry all day long, while on others they are giggling and playing, and appear happy and cozy. What that means is that you *have a right to feel "off" on some days, but that doesn't mean that that will last forever, and it certainly doesn't mean that you're a failure.*

Ann had difficulty relaxing and her anxiety often manifested through perfectionism. Here is what she learned through out work together:

"I've learned not to be so hard on myself and live judgement-free. If a task doesn't get done, it will be there waiting for me tomorrow and that is ok. If I am confronted with a situation that is out of my control, I remind myself that it's ok not to be in control, and that keeps me from 'beating' myself up about it."

–Ann

STOP BOTTLING UP!

One of the worst things you can do to yourself is to bottle up your feelings. What is worse than that is to continue bottling them up for a long time. Many of us carry feelings from years ago, even our childhood, that we never spoke about for various reasons. Either we were afraid or raised in a way that we never talk about home life and family problems, or we were ashamed, didn't feel comfortable, or had no support to share our story with. Until very recently, people were wary of therapy in general, and speaking about problems was considered weakness (believe it or not, I still hear that from some people today). These are all the reasons that factor in development of anxiety, depression and the like. Collecting anger, sadness, even only words that you never spoke up when you felt that somebody was being unfair to you, all lead to long term problems like anxiety. I can't tell you how often my clients come in and vent throughout the entire session, processing feelings on their own, only to say at the end, "Wow, this felt good! I feel better!" No, I don't have a magic wand to "make anybody better" in one session, sometimes I barely say a few words of validation; but venting is what my clients need and what makes them feel better instantly.

When we talk about our feelings, worries, fear, and anxieties, they no longer have the power over us. If they are kept inside, they multiply, grow stronger, and take over control. If we face them, speak them out loud, and free ourselves from them, we take over – we are the ones in control. Letting go of those feelings that were bottling up for so long, and finally feeling free and as if we took off a heavy rock off of our chest, is therapeutic in itself. If you were ever my client, you have heard me say, "If you don't feel 10 lbs. lighter when you leave here, we're not doing something right!"

If you were ever my client, you most likely also know my feelings metaphors. One of them being *the Coke bottle* (talk about bottling). When I use this metaphor, I want to explain to my clients how feelings turn into anxiety. Imagine a Coke bottle that is full to the top. And then imagine that you keep shaking and shaking and shaking. Will the bottle eventually "explode?" Will all the Coke burst out through the top of the bottle, sending cap through the roof? Most likely. YOU are that bottle. And if you keep triggering and shaking your feelings, while you are still trying to push down any more of them, there is only so much you can handle. Bursting of that bottle is what your anxiety feels like. It escapes your body uncontrollably in the form of irritability, crying, sadness, anger, fear, panic… Keep emptying your bottle whenever you can, and never let it fill up to the top.

Another example I often mention relates to carrying feelings; both yours and those of others. Taking on worries of the world on your backs, thinking about your friends' troubles, your family members', as if you don't have enough of your own… Thinking about everybody's relationships, health, whether they have taken their medication, what did they say about you, why did they have an argument with another family member, whether your child is late home despite the curfew, whether they have a problem in school, whether you like your child's significant other, what is your spouse doing when spending time on their phone… If you are one of those people, it is very likely that you're carrying too many suitcases; many of those not belonging to you. Imagine walking and carrying your backpack. Your child comes and brings you their suitcase. Your spouse brings another one. Your friend hands you a bag. Your parents give you another one. Along the way, more people hand you additional bags. How long will it take for you until you break? Until you can't carry anymore, and you fall down?

When you finally fall down, that is called an anxiety attack. You have carried so many feelings with you that you cannot handle any more of them.

CHARGE YOUR "PHONE"

The sentence that I hear the most from my clients of all ages whenever we talked about self-care is, "I don't have time!" followed by the long list of things they *have to* do, people they *have to* worry about. Breaking news everyone! You don't *have to* anything! You *want to*! Yes, I understand that your children, your parents, your younger siblings, your partners, your students, your clients, your pets, all require some care, but have you ever wondered how much giving you can do before completely and utterly draining yourself? I always remind my clients (and honestly, myself too), that we need to take care of ourselves in order to be able to take care of others.

Giving is a beautiful thing, but a very draining one. Taking on responsibilities for others, your own chores, your work, cleaning, cooking, babysitting, studying… is a lot! And yes, it does take a lot of time, but what doesn't? I read a quote somewhere yesterday, that read something along the lines of, "You will never find time, you have to MAKE time." So true! The time is not laying around, waiting for you to use it. And be true to yourself, even if that was the case, would you use it for relaxation, or get hyped about another errand that you have time to run, another room to clean, or another chapter of the textbook to read in advance of your next class? I will take a wild guess that it will be the second option. Why do we do that? We are so immersed in expectations of the society we live in to work hard, to put in more hours at work, to be at the top of our class, to run as many errands as we can, to make more money… But, do we ever live? When do we take the time to reap the benefits of that hard work? When do we really stop and smell those roses? Sit on the park bench without having the phone in our hand and just look around appreciating nature, and listening to the sounds of the birds? Rarely ever. And even if we do, it's "to kill time" until our lunch hour expires, until the bus arrives, until friend meets us. Don't kill that time, use it as best as you can. Use it productively and use it in such a way that it will remind you to appreciate life more, to count your blessings and enjoy every free moment that you can. That is one way to practice self-care.

As you may have an idea by now, I am big on metaphors, and I will gladly use another one here to prove my point. I'm sure that you have a cell phone, maybe you're an Apple lover, maybe an Android, but what I'm going to say, they both have in common – they need to be *charged*. We use our phones excessively throughout the day; to call, to text, to check our e-mails, to post on social media, to take photos, to edit photos, to listen to music, to play CandyCrush, you name it! But, to do all of that, the phone needs to be charged. The same way that you give your phone a break while charging it, give yourself some time to charge yourself. You are as active as your phone, if not even more, therefore, you need to give yourself a break from time to time in order to be able to do everything you want successfully, and to be able to help others. For those of you who are having a hard time accepting this, as I know there are many, think of it this way – you *have to* take care of yourself, so you can be healthy and functional to help those around you and get things done. If you don't take a break from time to time, the likelihood is, you will burn out and you could get sick, or be so drained that you will be of no use for yourself or others. And if that happens – nothing gets done. Point is, selfcare is not optional!

VALUE OF A MINUTE

Hand-in-hand with what I talked about before, time management is key. And making time for self-care is crucial, along with organizing your time in a most productive manner conducive to finishing what needs to get done as effectively, and in the least stressful way possible. In previous chapters I talked about various lists and planners that help you stay on track with your time and responsibilities, and in that way help keep your anxiety in check. We talked about organizing time, but how do we use that time efficiently? How can we multitask and ensure that we're accomplishing what we intended, but also learning how to manage time in such a way that those tasks do not become overbearing for us?

Time is very valuable, and often, we do not understand the length of a minute. My whole life I thought, "I only have 5 minutes, there is no way to get anything done, I'll just wait for (insert activity) and do it later." And then, I became a therapist. And I learned how important that minute is, and how much it can mean to a person. My clients can share a lot in just a few minutes, I can give them a suggestion or feedback in that one minute that could significantly improve their week. I could help them do breathing exercises for a minute at the end of the session, and have them leave feeling more relaxed and comfortable. I could discuss their next appointment. Outside of the session, I also find those minutes to be very important. When I have a few minutes in between two sessions, I could use them to have a small snack and re-charge my batteries, I could do a 2-minute guided meditation to help myself "cleanse" from my previous sessions, and prepare for the upcoming ones. I could return a phone call, or respond to an important text message or e-mail. I could run to the restroom. I could text my loved one to check on their day, or read a nice message from them that will give me more positive energy for the rest of the day. There is a lot you can do in a minute.

Most of these activities that I mentioned involve some sort of self-care, did you notice? I mention them for a reason, to show you that you don't need 3 hours a day to practice self-care, you can do it in just a few minutes – and you can do it anywhere! You can do a short meditation or a breathing exercise at your office desk; you can also have a snack there. A couple of stretching exercises to stimulate your blood flow can be done in the bathroom in just a few seconds. A sweet text can be sent in a few seconds as well, and it takes only a couple of minutes to refresh in the restroom, wash your face, and feel a little more awake and alert.

I talk to students a lot about time management, and one of the things that I mention, that is also related to self-care in such a way that they save time and leave more room to do what they enjoy, is multitasking. By multitasking, I don't mean physically doing 3 things at once (in fact, I believe that that's anxiety provoking and it doesn't help you get much done; it even slows down the process), I mean utilizing time during which you believe you can't get much done, productively (just like those few minutes in between my sessions). One of the best examples is a train ride. We often complain about long transportation time that takes away from us doing x, y, and z. It would be nice if we looked at it from a different perspective, and thought of ways in which we can make that time more productive. For instance, if you are on your way home from school, use the transportation time to read your chapters for the next day, respond to your e-mails, call a friend, do a short guided meditation, and that in itself will help the time spent in public transportation seemingly shorter, but also allow you to have less tasks to complete when you arrive home, and give you more time to relax or do something else that needs to be done that you never seem to have time to do. If anything, you may at least bring yourself back on track in terms of school work, for instance, if you were backed up a little with some reading. This of course, does not apply to students only, as transportation time can be utilized productively in so many ways for those who are long out of school too. Use the time on the bus or train to call and schedule your appointments for instance; phone calls usually take up a lot of time that you could spend at home doing something else. Calling customer service for an issue that you need to resolve is also more productive if done on the train (you can also place the call on speaker and wait for the representative while cooking, cleaning or responding to e-mails, instead of waiting with the phone in your hand, which can only get you anxious about wasted time). Having your down time on the train is also helpful; you can meditate, read a book, read news, or scroll through social media while relaxing, so you have your batteries charged at least a little before you get home and dive into more work that's waiting for you.

Other than transportation, waiting rooms are an excellent environment for getting stuff done. Doctors' offices, bank consultations, hair salons... all those provide you with perfect "empty" time for you to fill in with productive activities. I've often advised my clients who were students to take their homework to the doctor's office, and they usually reported completing almost everything while waiting! That left room for them to see their friends after, watch movies, spend time with family, surf the internet, or engage in a hobby. For those of you who are no longer students, respond to work e-mails from the waiting room, read that book you've been trying to find the time for but kids, husbands, and cooking responsibilities prevented you, text a friend, write in a journal, organize your planner, or create lists that we discussed previously. You will feel a lot better about yourself and your day in general: more productive, more organized, less anxious, and definitely accomplished!

DECLUTTERING

Somebody once said, "Order in your life is order in your thoughts." Do you ever feel anxious when you walk into your home and it appears messy? When your clothes are not in their place, dishes are not washed, some plates or cups are stranded on tables and nightstands? When you get to your office and paperwork is not orderly, you have a huge to do list and have began working on each of the tasks but haven't fully completed any? When a bunch of Post-It notes are all over the place, and many of them have been long completed but never thrown?
I know I get anxious. I know some of my clients do. And I also know about simple ways to resolve this issue. Make a To Do List about things that need to be cleaned up, and spaces that need to be decluttered and start small.

Every couple of months, if not more frequently, I make an effort to declutter my closet and get rid of any of the clothes that no longer fit or I haven't worn in a long time. I know some of you might have emotional attachment to your clothes and belongings in general, and I do too. What helps me is that I remind myself that I could be doing a good deed, and therefore, I always donate all the clothes that are in good shape, and hope that they will keep someone comfortable and warm in the winter. Along with my closet, I clean out my paperwork. I review the drawer with documentation, and make sure that nothing that is not important hangs around there. Documents have expiration dates, and there is no reason to hold on to piles of paperwork that are completely useless.

When I talk about clutter, I don't only talk about "mess." I talk about cleanliness of the space in general, in terms of organization and placement of furniture and décor. If you are unhappy in your living space, your home is no longer a safe heaven, and it is very easy for it to become yet another trigger. That is why I strongly suggest for you to make changes to it according to your needs. If you are someone who enjoys clean, modern furniture pieces, who doesn't like too many things in their way, make your home clean and leave as much space open. If you are one of those people who, like myself, enjoy natural light, plants, beautiful works of art, include them in your living space to brighten it up and make it your own. Make your home truly your own, and enable yourself to feel safe, comfortable, and fully relaxed the moment you walk in.

We spend more time in our offices that we do in our homes, on most days. Therefore, office is another place to make comfortable and working for you, ability to do that permitting, of course. Even if you don't have your own office or are working in a shared space, bring something small but meaningful. I would bring small plants, a scented candle, or a quote that I could move around as necessary, and it greatly helped me in feeling as if the space belonged to me a little more.

If you have any old things that are useless, torn, chipped, if they are not particularly emotionally meaningful to you, get rid of them. Throw them out or put them in storage. Believe me, when there is no clutter around you, and when everything is in its place and you can locate it and clearly see where everything is and whether something needs a bit more of your attention, you will feel ten times more relaxed than in an opposite situation. You will not be overwhelmed with the mess you are looking at, as it usually appears larger in your mind than it is in your eyes. Keep your mind and space decluttered, and enjoy that awesome state of mind!

GET CREATIVE

Many of you who are reading this have amazing creative talents. Even if you are not the most artistic person in the world, I'm sure you are good at something and could use that *something* as an outlet. I talked about journals a lot, but I do understand that journals are not for everybody, especially not for those of you who dislike writing, or at least, not enjoy it. The good news is, you can find your own version of a journal, and utilize it accordingly. I have the pleasure of working with some people who are wonderful artists and whose work never fails to impress me. Their emotions are expressed in a beautiful way through art, imagination, and often, very subconsciously, tell a story that not even the author is aware of. Feelings, intentions, forgotten pains, and fears come through in their drawings, paintings, rap music, songs, and poems that they write. In sessions in which I use art as a form of expression, more often than not, some sort of epiphany is revealed.

Art is an amazing way to process emotions, express yourself, and feel proud with the end result. Along with processing feelings and learning about yourself, you get to do what you enjoy and work on your self-confidence at the same time. Your art will remain kept, and will always remind you of the long way that you've come, your growth, past experiences that you were able to overcome, but it will also serve as a reminder of where you are in the process, and help you set your healing goals. It will be a teller of what else you need to work on, what are the areas that need further improvement, and become an eye opener about what, in this process, do you find most challenging. If you are in therapy, art is a phenomenal way to begin the discussion, and your therapist will often utilize your art to help you express yourself if verbal expression is not the easiest task for you. Believe it or not, expressing feelings, and even identifying them properly, does not come easy to many people (including therapists!). Therefore, use your poems, drawings, paintings, play-doh, whatever it is that is your niche, to help you on your therapeutic journey!

Art can help you with a variety of emotions - pretty much all of them. It is a healthy way to express and release anger through use of motion, colors, shapes and themes that you find are related to what you're feeling. When you are anxious, it helps you focus, keep your hands busy, remain in the present moment, and refrain from engaging in negative and fearful thought processes. Drawing shapes and forms, coloring, and allowing yourself to fully let go and draw whatever is on your mind, is definitely a very soothing and calming activity.

Writing poems is also a wonderful way to put your feelings into words by describing them, rather than identifying them by utilizing one dry word that usually does not encompass everything that your heart holds. By allowing yourself to get lost in your imagination and dive into the depths of your heart and mind, you release your feelings, and end up feeling lighter and better because you have gotten your point across, and you never have to explain yourself again. Along with poems, you can write short stories, essays, or any other form of creative writing that is your cup of tea.

Recently, more and more clients are telling me that they

enjoy writing rap music. I want to thank them this way, because that is the genre that I have never thought of suggesting (I think I have mentioned that I love learning from and with my clients, because they are the best teachers!). Rap is particularly great with teenagers, as that is the popular music that they can relate to nowadays, and it allows them to express themselves in the language that they use daily and are familiar with. To be fair, it also sounds less of a chore and less frightening to write a rap song, rather than a poem, which does give out a connotation of seriousness and responsibility. Whatever the case, and regardless of your preference, utilizing any form of creative writing is a perfect way to put your feelings into words that are unique to you, and really encompass what is it that you are really feeling, deep down.

Knitting and needle point have been very popular especially among female portion of my clients. Both of these art forms help you focus and reduce symptoms of anxiety, while they also help you feel accomplished and creative. As I might have mentioned before, anxiety exits through hands (which is why, every time we're anxious, we reach for our phone and keep clicking between Facebook and Instagram, we feel the need to punch something, etc.), and knitting and needle point target exactly that. They channel your energy to the right passage ways, and help you to safely, and productively, cope with your feelings. Their end products could also keep you warm in the winter!

Any other form of art is welcome and you cannot go wrong. DIY (Do It Yourself) projects, plenty of which you can find on websites such as Pinterest, are another great way to put your creative juices to use and have them assist you in your battle with feelings. They are also very cute and functional, therefore, they will end up serving multiple purposes. Building and making something, using play-doh, blocks, creating bouquets with real or artificial flowers (as I call it, "gardening"), making scrap books, organizing and collecting stickers, photos, or cooking recipes, are all ideas that you can utilize in your battle against anxiety. These are only some of the creative strategies that I am suggesting, however I am certain that you are way more creative and can find your own niche that I could not even think of at this moment. This is what helped my long-term client:

"Many people unfortunately choose a self-destructive route to cope with emotions, but I learned a more productive way. I use my creativity as an outlet to let out my emotions in a more positive way. I love to draw, paint, rap and write, to fully let go of my emotions. It is through my art that I can also allow others to experience exactly what I am feeling and have a better understanding of it. I have changed and touched the lives of many with my art, and that is something that I am very passionate about, it's a great feeling. It's as if I don't have to carry that negativity anymore, I'm free and it's amazing that I was able to learn more about using my passion as a coping strategy."

–Genesis Abreu

COLORING BOOKS

I know you're not a kid, but hear me out! Adult coloring books are an amazing way to de-stress and cope with your anxiety. They are a perfect way to focus, remain in the moment, and allow for your stress to exit through your hands and be absorbed by the paper. Coloring books help you improve focus and concentration, which are, in most cases, greatly impacted by anxiety, and to let go of your emotions. Buy a coloring book, get some pretty color pencils, and keep it within reach!

VISUALIZATION

In recent years, visualization became the word that we hear more and more often, almost daily. Law of attraction has become an increasingly popular topic, and with it, many ideas about different ways to manifest your wishes found their way to the public. I am sure that some of you are skeptical about whether manifestations and visualizations work, but bear with me for a moment, as they could prove to be useful in your treatment. I will not go into too much depth on this topic, as it is not something that I have intended for the purpose of this book, however,

I do believe that it is worth mentioning, and here is why.

The piece that I utilized in my work with clients, and that has stemmed from my reading of "The Secret," was the *vision board* and a *wish list* (I have read about this in multiple other books as well, one of them being "Write It Down, Make It Happen" by Henriette Klauser that I highly recommend). What is important to mention before I go deeper into talking about this, is that wish lists and vision boards are not miracle workers. You should never write down your list of wishes, and do nothing about them – instead, you should take them as what they truly are – *your goals*. When you write your goals down, you solidify them. You know what you want, and you should now start to work on a plan on how to get there. This is one of the excellent ways to alleviate your anxiety, as it allows you to see a clear picture of what you want and how to get there on paper. Breaking down your goals into smaller steps is key; looking at the big picture often creates anxiety for many of us, and more often than not, either brings us to doubting ourselves and our abilities, or gets us to completely give up as the goal seems so big and unattainable, so far out of reach. Breaking it down into smaller steps, makes it more "human," more doable and closer to us. Remember when you were in school and had a test to take? When you shuffled through pages, saw a hundred of them, glanced at the clock, and thought, "Oh my, there is no way I have enough time to finish all of this," and then started to become anxious and overwhelmed? I certainly remember those chest-tightening moments. What I learned after, and now try to share with my student clients, is to break the test down and focus only on what's in front of them. Cover up all the other questions, and focus only on the one you are working on. Then do the same for the next one, and the next one, and the next one… That way you allow yourself to increase concentration, focus on the here and now, and boost confidence after getting questions done one by one, and having less and less left to do. When it comes to goal-setting, I advise you to take that same approach.

Writing of this book has been on my mind for a very long time. At first, I was unsure about the topic, then I thought about how would I go about it, how to break it down, and finally, where to begin and how to tackle on all the aspects I wanted to address. Was it too big of a bite for me to chew? Did I have enough experience to write this kind of a book? Was I good enough to write it? And finally, when I do, would I be able to publish it, and then who would read it? All those doubts were on my mind, and the book seemed too big of an accomplishment to start on. The idea of publishing it, and the final result sounded amazing, but getting there was tough.

Until one day, I just started. I grabbed my lap top, went to my room, got cozy in my bed and typed up my intro. I didn't pay attention to what it was like, whether it was all I imagined it to be, but I typed and said to myself that this is only the first draft, and I am being playful. Word by word, sentence by sentence, I finally got to page by page and finished my first chapter. I was so proud, and I was so excited to see that it was flowing and that I had so much to say! I created an outline prior to beginning to write, and kept adding more and more to it. I always had it handy, and whenever I would remember something that could be useful, I'd drop in a bullet point on that notepad. My outline soon started to make sense, and the material was enough to get me to about a hundred pages, which was amazing. I first set smaller goals to myself; I'd write 2 pages a day. I'd write 10 pages a week. Then it got to the point that I was so engaged with my writing, that I would have my lap top handy, and would drop in a sentence (that would usually turn into a couple of pages) almost every time I passed by it. My large, anxiety-provoking goal, became manageable, as I took small steps towards it almost every day. Brick by brick eventually builds a wall.

Approach your life struggles in the same way as I approached writing of this book. Whenever you can, get some support. I can't fail to mention a wonderful lady who has helped with my motivation after I started slacking with writing due to a busy schedule at work. I met Laurie through Instagram, and her video in which she invited people to create an accountability group that would help them achieve a goal in two weeks, helped kick start what could have ended up being a failed attempt at a book that would end up sitting in my lap top for the next few years, untouched (like some chapters that are already doing that). Laurie became my accountability buddy, and I set my goal to twenty pages in two weeks. Laurie and I updated one another on our progress daily, and along with our accomplishments, also talked to one another about missing out on our tasks at times and reasons for it. I learned a lot about forgiveness of self through this project, and Laurie encouraged me to give myself a pat on the back for even the smallest accomplishment. I learned that an outline, as well as thinking about and planning, count as progress towards the goal. It was comforting knowing that I have support, and it felt motivating to have somebody to report to; I felt as if I was betraying the project and could not e-mail my update without getting anything done. It was embarrassing to say the least, and in the best way possible. You are now thinking that I got those twenty pages done and added a few more on top, don't you? I did not get twenty pages done, but I did twelve. Which was still better than nothing, and it helped me get back on track. I did not accomplish my goal when I expected to, but I still got more done than I would have had I not joined Laurie's group, and I got twelve pages closer to it. Thank you, Laurie, for being such wonderful support!

No matter what it is that you are working on, no matter whether your goal is writing a book, getting over your anxiety, finding your dream job, buying a new car, becoming an acknowledged artist, or being a great mom, break down those goals into smaller steps, and write them all down on pieces of paper, or put them up on a pin board. Watch as each of those steps are coming true, and evolving towards development of your dream. Make sure to grab some awesome support on the way, and report your progress to them. Get somebody who will be full of joy over the smallest of your accomplishments, who will give you a pat on the back, but who will also be there to motivate and encourage you when you're not at your best. Have them remind you that you are only human, and that not every day will be as productive as the one before, or the one after. Along the way, learn to forgive yourself. Learn to give yourself credit for your hard work, even if that means "only" brainstorming about your goal. Isn't brainstorming how every great idea started? Brainstorming is on the other end of your accomplished goal – walk that line with confidence.

PHYSICAL ACTIVITY

I'm sure you all have, at some point in your lives, read about benefits of physical activity, or were talked to by your doctors and teachers. Besides physical health, physical activity has amazing benefits on your mental health. You have heard of dopamine, endorphin, and other "happy hormones and chemicals," that improve your mood and make you feel better. It has been scientifically proven that physical activity does have great positive impact on our bodies, and that it helps in treatment of depression and anxiety greatly.

Walking, in particular, assists in improving your mood, while also allowing you to "clear your head," be mindful, and free yourself from negative thoughts and feelings. Breathing properly and walking with nice, straight up posture, additionally help in improvement of your mood. If you, in addition, remain mindful, focus on your surroundings without allowing your thoughts to drift away to your anxieties, and possibly have guided meditation coming through your headphones, that would be a winning combination for full, deep relaxation, and therapeutic walk.

Any other type of exercise, whether it being at home or at the gym, is excellent. Sweating, and allowing energy to exit your body, helps tremendously in letting go of negative feelings. Exercise is one of the strategies that my client found the most suitable for herself and which she practices daily, especially during periods of high stress.

"I enjoy exercising, it makes me feel better about myself, puts me
In a better mood and gives me energy I didn't have before.
So I have committed to working out at least 4 times a week.
When I feel the pressure of anxiety rising, I put on my workout
gear and workout. It gets the endorphins going, relieves the
pressure, and clears my mind from stress and anxiety."

–Ann

Exercise, especially the kind that utilizes arms and hands, such as punching bags, sports like tennis or volleyball, and even swimming, are especially great for releasing anger and anxiety. Do you notice that when you are upset you feel like punching something? There is that powerful energy flowing through your arms and hands, and it almost feels like you will explode unless you release it? That build up is often so intense, that people have trouble controlling it, and succumb to punching walls, breaking expensive objects, and sometimes even punching others. That is why I highly recommend engaging in physical activity and letting go of energy through productive use of hands. Remember Joshua from the chapter on journaling? He shared with you about how sport has been helpful to him as well:

"…the best way of getting over my anxiety is physical activity; in my case handball. It helps me get a lot of frustration and extra energy that I have due to anxiety out. Handball is a very fun and effective way for me to stay calm and not overthink."

–Joshua Mercado

During my early studies of psychology, I learned from a professor that many athletes have anger issues. However, there is a difference between them, and those who have ended up incarcerated – athletes are utilizing their anger in constructive, healthy ways. Anger, as a component of anxiety, could be a very powerful force in helping you feel better and overcoming these troublesome symptoms, if you only use it right. I often recommend a stress ball to my clients with anxiety and anger problems, and quite frequently, I hear that it didn't work, and they got even more anxious or angry. Why is that? It's all about the mindset and the thought process. If you go into the exercise of squeezing the stress ball, your mind must absolutely be set on "I am releasing my feelings into this ball" (that you could imagine as a sponge collecting your negative feelings), rather than "I am imagining this person who made me angry, and hurting them back" – this one is a no-no, not helpful. Those of you who go into it having that second thought process, experience increase in anger and/or anxiety, not vice versa. However, those who visualize anger as energy flowing through the body, and with each hand motion, coming out through hands, helping the release of it, those are the ones who are doing a good job. Again, make sure to maintain full, deep breaths while doing so, and to focus on letting go and wanting to feel better.

One of my favorite physical activities to practice and talk about is yoga. Yoga has been becoming increasingly popular in recent years, and I've gotten more and more curious. I liked to imagine benefits of yoga and meditation, and feel impressed by those able to maintain that lifestyle; the problem was, I could not stick to any of it long enough to really reap the real benefits, or become a knowledgeable expert in them. However, at the right time, even this has changed. I am now a firm believer that both yoga and meditation stuck with me once I was ready for them, and went into practices for the right reasons. Earlier in the book, I talked to you about my journey with *Calm*, and how much it has helped me to commit to meditation practice. It only took the right match for me to be able to believe it, buy into it, and have (once again) that **mindset** that meditation will help me. Similar scenario happened with yoga, here is how.

Somehow, I was always more inclined to do yoga than meditation, and the reason why is because I am a very jittery person, who cannot sit still. I'm sure many of you feel the same, and you are free to choose what is your favorite coping strategy, what is most comfortable for you, and most importantly, which one you are most likely to stick to. Ideally, you would practice both meditation and yoga, as they go hand in hand in many ways, but even one of them could provide unbelievable benefits. I've done yoga a few times in my life over the course of a few years, mostly watching YouTube videos, and sticking to the one I kind of-sort of like, until I become bored of it and stopped altogether. I've had difficulty finding a yogi that will meet my interests and my physical agility – some videos were too slow, to the point where I'd yawn and get really sleepy very close to the beginning (which wasn't bad if I was doing it at night before going to bed), while others would be too advanced, and I'd focus on attempting to do a pose to the point where I'd forget to breathe properly, or I'd even miss half of the video because I waited for a less advanced pose to come up. And then, last spring, I came across Adrianne.

One evening I was scrolling through YouTube videos, looking for a short and sweet one that will be a quick fix for my neck and back pain. I came across *Yoga with Adrianne* and loved that video, which lead me to exploring more of her channel, and learning about an amazing variety of her practices. Her *30 Day Challenge* popped up, and I decided to go for it (I even had an accountability buddy, thank you Sophie!). Needless to say how much I learned, and how helpful this challenge was. Not only did I learn about yoga, proper breathing, and importance of allowing your body to guide you, but I learned about myself. I reached new limits and changed some habits. For instance, I was never the one to engage in any self-care prior to going to work in the afternoon – during this challenge, I made an effort to wake up earlier to do yoga and meditate before going to work, and I actually enjoyed it!

When doing yoga, it is important to remain in tune with

your body; to extend yourself only as much as it's comfortable. Focusing on the breathing and maintaining nice, deep, steady breaths, allows you to reach new limits and expand your body in ways you never thought would be possible. While you are doing yoga, you are actually meditating, how awesome is that? With each yoga practice, you are reducing stress and anxiety, and replenishing on energy; yoga increases motivation and gives you positive energy to carry throughout the day. It is an amazing stretch, and helps work out various kinks in the body, particularly those of the spinal, back, and neck pains (it even helps you get rid of a migraine due to improved circulation!). I'm sure that I have missed out on a whole lot of benefits, which I am going to leave up to you to learn about and explore, but I will mention one last, but certainly not the least, benefit that is my personal favorite – doing yoga slows time down. You are there, in the moment, there is no past, there is no future, there is only you, your body and your breath, part of the infinite space that becomes one with you and helps you feel strong, confident, and secure. Sounds beautiful, right? It's also real, go try it.

SUPPORT

Lastly, I feel obligated to write a little about importance of the support system. Anxiety is a terrible disease that is not easy to cope with alone. You need a good, supportive army of those who understand it, who understand you, and who are able to provide space for you to process feelings, and become motivators for your coping strategies. Ensure that you educate your loved ones on anxiety, or bring them to your therapy sessions. I love inviting my clients' family members and significant others join us in sessions, so they can learn more about what anxiety is, what my clients are going through, and ask any questions that they might have. I make suggestions about ways in which they can support and help my clients, while also protecting themselves from feeling exasperated and burnt out from the role of a caretaker. These meetings greatly help in increase of understanding, learning, and strengthening the bond between the person with anxiety and their caretaker.

For those of you who are struggling with symptoms, please do not hesitate to speak about it. Be honest about your feelings and how scary your thought processes are for you. Do not feel ashamed to seek support or call for help when you need somebody to hold your hand. Healthy and honest communication is key in gaining the healthy support system, be it by significant others, friends, or family members. The more understanding they gain from you, the more they will be in tune with your needs and their abilities to help you.

POWER OF THE WILL

Throughout this book, I addressed plenty of coping strategies that could be of help to you, anxiety or not. They are not only good in treatment of anxiety, but serve as excellent self-care activities for all of us. The one key ingredient for every one of these strategies is the **willpower**. You must want to help yourself make positive changes to your life, and you must enjoy what you engage in. I attempted going to the gym so many times, but was never successful, never lasted more than a few days – why? Because it is not my cup of tea. However, when I do meditation – I feel at home. It works for me, I find it working well with my schedule, and I don't find it to be a chore; I actually look forward to doing it. And that is the true reason to do something, and *that* is why it works.

I always encourage my clients to try different things and find what works for them. I am big on asking about their hobbies and interests, and make suggestions based off of those. If my client is an athlete, guess what I might recommend. If they are an artist – you know it! But if they are unsure of what might work for them, I suggest a few different options, and they test-drive them. It cannot hurt, one just might work better than the other, so do not hesitate to explore, you might even surprise yourself with something that you never expected will work. In addition, let your therapist know what worked and what didn't. I usually utilize that information to explore *why* certain activities did not work, and why others do, which often provides crucial information towards their treatment.

CLOSING REMARKS

Writing this book has been my dream, as working with anxiety and seeing progress and lifechanging experiences of my clients, is my passion. Anxiety is something that I know very well, and something that has been a big part of my life for a few years. I learned about it not only from college textbooks and my work with clients, but from first-hand experiences and my mother's struggle. My life mission is to help those who are in the same boat, and provide them with tools to use to make their lives as quality as possible. My hope is that this book will help supplement the work that I do inside the office, but also, to reach those who are struggling but are unable to seek treatment for whatever reason. I hope this book helps all of you that I have a special bond with as you share the struggle with my mother, who is today, anxiety-free. And at the end, before I click "Save" on my lap top and send this over to an agent that I hope will like it, there is someone who would like to say a few words to you.

"Anxiety" – that word scared me a lot 4 years ago. At the mention of it, I'd feel fear building inside of me, fear that I will never get rid of it. First message I must send out to all of you is that the person who is dealing with anxiety cannot think like that! There is a solution always and for everything. Anxiety could be beat. When I first began realizing, and finally understood completely, that anxiety is some sort of my unrealistic fear, I freed myself from it completely. I began to live normally, ride the train, walk by myself, take plan rides. Everything that I was afraid to even think of doing. A lot of meditation, healthy eating, exercising, all that helps in one's fight against anxiety. I think positive, I avoid negative people. Life is beautiful, don't spend it feeling anxious! Do not allow that stubborn and annoying illness to ruin and hurt your body. Be stronger than it. Even now, after such a long time, when I deal with situations that are exciting, that worry me, anxiety tries to creep in, silently, unnoticeably. But I send it away with my positive thinking, strongly believing that one could find an exit from every unpleasant situation, that there is a solution for everything! Beat anxiety, if I did it, you can too!

Love,
Vesna